Speak From Within

Engage, Inspire, and Motivate Any Audience

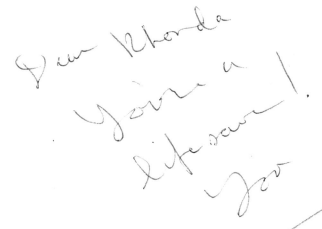

IZOLDA TRAKHTENBERG

ISBN: 0-9802298-9-8
ISBN-13: 978-0-9802298-9-9

DEDICATION

To the storytellers, the truth-speakers, and the weavers of dreams.

To my students.

.

CONTENTS

ACKNOWLEDGMENTS

I'm grateful to the following people without whose help this book would not exist.

My husband Rich Potter: For your wisdom, laughter, and love.

To my mom Ida Kogan, my sisters Emily Altman and Golda Noble, and my sister from another mister, my best friend Kristen Hughes Evans: for your unwavering love and guidance

To my beta readers: T.S.R. Gallagher, Leigh Johnson, Adrienne Adler Kerbel, Debi Brady, Lee Morey, Kathy Zottmann, Eric Henning, Mechell Dickens, Brecken Chinn, Heather Weir, and Teanna Byerts: for your insights, wisdom, and ideas.

To my incredible teachers: Mary Alice Powell, Linda Gutman, Kathryn Wolak, and Marian Littman. Thank you for encouraging me to stretch my wings as a reader, writer, speaker and teacher.

To the CEG: Rich Potter, Eric Henning, Patty Hill, Dayle Hodge, Lee Morey, and Charon Henning: Thank you! You know why.

To my amazing editor and dear friend, Petra Mayer: Your wisdom, guidance, and attention to detail elevated this book beyond my wildest dreams.

To Mr. Red: for this fantastic cover and to William Cornett for my lovely author photo. Stunning work.

Last, I want to thank you. I hope you have gotten what you needed and had some fun throughout the process. When you have the courage to speak your truth, you transform your life and the lives of everyone who hears you. Particularly, if you picked this book up to banish public speaking fears, I thank you for having the courage to do it. That took guts. So, good for you and thank you.

INTRODUCTION

"Now, what shall we talk about?"

One dozen chocolate chip cookies to the first three people who can name the movie that line is from. (I'm not kidding: The first three people who contact me with their correct guess – without looking below for the answer – and send me their address will get a package of chocolate chip cookies).

Did you guess *Raiders of the Lost Ark*? If so, you got it! The evil Major Arnold Toht says it to Marion Ravenwood, right as he's about to torture her for information. He says the words in a benign tone, but we all know he is anything but benign.

The way actor Ronald Lacey says that little bit of friendly-seeming text sends a shiver through both the audience and the other actors in the scene. It's a moment of inspired storytelling.

Anytime we recount something that happened, we tell a story about it. If we wonder what might happen, we also tell a story – even if it's only in our own heads. It might be a literary tale or one of great adventure like *Raiders of the Lost Ark*, but each time we talk, we tell a tale. And every tale we tell has a description, action, and some sort of conclusion.

Since we all tell stories, why is it that many of us balk at the idea of dubbing ourselves storytellers or crafters of tales? Why are so many of us hesitant to call ourselves writers or communicators?

Let's imagine an elder by the bonfire, regaling the youngsters of the village with ancient myths of heroes and monsters or the reason for the seasons or stories about how the world came to be. It sounds fabulous, doesn't it? It makes me wistful and nostalgic all at the same time. What a glorious picture.

But the trouble with that picture is that it seems like only that exalted elder can be trusted to spin such a tale and make it exciting and engaging. We all have the impulse to express ourselves, but somewhere along the line, many of us picked up the dubious notion that we can't or shouldn't be storytellers – and that's a tragedy. I believe we all have the right and even a duty to share our stories. Otherwise, how will the world know us? We must tell our stories to our community, and with the Internet, our community is the whole world.

Social media platforms offer opportunities to tell stories in written, verbal, photographic, and video form. So, if you use communication of any sort for social media, for your profession, or just to let your mom know you'll be home late, chances are you are a communicator, a writer, a creator, and a teller of tales.

I believe communication is our birthright. Remember, what is the first thing we do when we're born? We scream. We have no thought that perhaps we shouldn't. We have no idea that perhaps no one wants to hear it. We don't care. We have a story to tell, and we tell it as best we can with the tools we have. Somewhere along the line, we lose that notion, but

I'm here to help us all get it back.

I've always thought that babies come out of the womb knowing the secret to life. Their trouble is that they speak a different language than most of the rest of us do. And I have a feeling that first cry is one of frustration, as we realize we aren't going to be able to make ourselves understood for months, or perhaps years.

Let's face it: Being understood, being heard, or being listened to – those are three important aspects of being alive and of our connection to those around us. It makes sense, then, that the people who hear you, understand you, and get you are the ones who end up closest to your heart and become your best friends.

Reclaiming that birthright will be a lot of work. I recommend you find a partner and work through the book together. Heck, start a group so you can practice communicating with – and in front of – each other. Plus, we tend to distrust our own ears, so it helps to have someone else as a sounding board. If you get stuck on something, contact me. Ask your questions and if I can answer, I will.

Having said that, if you decide to go through this book as a solo practitioner, that works great too. You'll need to look deep inside yourself to build the awareness of the changes that take place within you as you progress. After all, this entire process is a treasure hunt to find our true voices. Once you locate this particular treasure, you can break through any fears you might have about speaking in public and become a confident, engaging, and inspiring communicator.

Surveys and polls routinely find public speaking ranked close to the top of people's fears. They place public speaking right up there with being the victim of identity theft or a mass shooting. People fear standing up in front of others to communicate almost as much as they fear death or government corruption (https://blogs.chapman.edu/press-room/2014/10/20/what-americans-fear-most-new-poll-from-chapman-university/). That makes me sad in a way I find hard to describe. We all have insights and ideas worth sharing and how awful that so many shrink away from sharing theirs.

I'm here to say it doesn't have to be that way. We do not have to be afraid of connecting and communicating with others. That's why I've written this book: It's time to lay those fears to rest, because we all deserve to be heard. And the key to being heard, to being a storyteller and a communicator, is to accept that mantle and tell your tales.

To do that, we must master a few other skills – first, listening and knowing what our listeners want to hear, and second, learning how to engage our audience. Then, whatever tale we tell them, they can't wait to hear more. Those two skills alone make up a great part of becoming a grand storyteller. With this book, you'll learn how to join their ranks.

This book is interactive. To help you get the most out of these ideas, I will be giving you missions – little exercises you can do on your own – throughout. I will also provide links to videos and other supplemental materials. If you are reading the print version of the book, please copy https://IzoldaT.com/speak-book into a browser for the resources and other supplemental materials. Together, these materials will help you build the skills and confidence to tell your stories with ease.

Are you ready? Let's get this party started!

1 EXPRESSION

Try this quick *mission*.

Mission: "I love you."

Say the words, "I love you," three times. The first time, emphasize the "I." The second time, stress the "love." The third time emphasize, the "you." Do those changes make what you're saying sound different? What sort of story might you tell with the first one? Two people are vying for the love of a third, and each is trying to convince her to choose them.

The second might be a tale of a romance where a couple has been bickering the entire time, until one finally yells, "I LOVE you," in frustration. What do you think the third might tell us? Certainly, the interpretation is up to the individual person. In my mind, an emphasis on the "you," indicates that the listener is the one the speaker **chose** above all others.

See what I mean? We get three radically different stories with just a bit of different emphasis.

A world of information can come through in a rising pitch or an emphasized word. We can see evidence of this

1

immediately, by paying attention to common phrases and how differently we can say them.

So, how we tell our story matters just as much, if not more, than what we say. And that's important because we are all storytellers! Every one of us is a spinner of tales. We are like those elders by the ancient bonfires, who taught the people of the village with their voices and their stories. Sure, we do it in different ways and for different reasons, but we all do it.

Yet, for many, the idea of telling any story daunts us. We shrink away from self-expression.

"No one will want to hear what I have to say," Samantha says to herself.

"I suck at this stuff," Mike complains.

"I don't have a talent for writing, speaking, singing, painting, drawing, etc." Deb confides. They have all convinced themselves they will be terrible at speaking in public.

Do you want to know what I have to say to that? Bull baloney. Yep, you read that right. Bull baloney.

We were born to express ourselves. I mean every word of that last statement. Self-expression is our birthright. What is the first thing we do when we come out of the birth canal?

We take a deep breath.

What is the second thing?

We scream. We express ourselves. Sure, it comes out as a cry or wail. But we "announce our presence with authority" (to quote another favorite movie from the '80s, and yes, another dozen cookies if you're the first to know which movie).

We don't wait for an invitation. We don't wonder if anyone wants to hear it. We don't shy away from a thing. We open our mouths, and we let it rip. We don't fear it. We just do it.

As we get older, that completely irrepressible self-expression gets more limited. And so when I say it's our birthright, that's because I think we all have the right to express ourselves from the very first second we're born. But then, we develop language, and we have to figure out how to communicate in such a way that others will take it the way we intend, and our message will achieve its goal.

So, that expressive birthright becomes more complicated and less effective. We forget that at our core, we are communicating beings – but if we remember that fact and apply it, we can transform our lives.

Many of us feel like speaking in public is torture, but I am here to tell you that it can be fun and exciting. You can have a terrific time speaking in front of people. I promise.

When it comes to public speaking, one of the things we have lost is that sense of fun and spontaneity. We live in a culture of judgment and immediate evaluation and perhaps even scorn; instead of support or constructive critique, people expect to be judged and found lacking. But what if things were different? What if instead of expecting and fearing derision, we went in with no expectations whatsoever? What if we left it open to connection? What if we went in with a sense of the fun we were all about to have together? Do you think that set of thoughts might change how our audience receives and perceives us? And more importantly, would that change how we perceive ourselves?

Certainly, at birth, we have no thought of – and no way to think about – being judged. No infant cares that they are naked. No infant worries about how they might look or sound. They simply exist in that moment and they express themselves fully and immediately. And with that sort of purity, the vast majority of the people who hear them can't help but reply and do whatever it takes to address the infant's needs.

I'm not saying we should scream, cry, or whimper for that attention and engagement. I'm saying we need to be present with those who are about to hear us. If we are present, real, and authentic, we will connect faster and go deeper with anyone who hears us. They will listen because our authenticity will strike a chord within them. And together we'll find that connection to the core of who we are. Therein lies the magic. If we can get *there*, we can take our audience anywhere we want to go. Why? Because they will want to come! They will delight in joining us on the journey. We are going to offer them the coolest adventure across the most wondrous landscape, the mystery of our authentic selves and our innate and thrilling connection to each other. Who wouldn't want to join that expedition?

What stops most of us from being that authentic? What keeps us from embarking on the expedition to explore our inner landscape so that we can connect with others on that primal level? If we broke that question down to its basic level, likely, it's fear.

That is the long and short of it. We are afraid. And if we admit the fear, then let's be courageous enough to ask the follow-up question. What on Earth are we afraid of? Take a second and think about it. What is truly the worst that could happen? What if our worst fears about public speaking and communication came true? What would happen then?

2 FEAR

Let's talk about fear. What happens when we are afraid?

First, there are the physical sensations of fear. We sweat. Our breathing intensifies. We might even pant. Our eyes might begin to dart around us. Our motions and movements become jerky, fast, and frantic. The butterflies in our stomachs launch into a jitterbug. Do those sound familiar? It's not surprising. Those are the very things the body does in order to prepare for a fight or flight response.

Our heart beats faster. Our cooling system jumps into action. Our breath heaves fast into our lungs so the muscles and blood become oxygenated and ready for action. We look around us to make sure we know what's going on, to ensure we know where the danger lies. We look for incongruities in our landscape. Are there hazards? Does everything seem OK? If not, we're ready for action. So, if those are the precursors to a fight or flight response, why do so many of us report that those are the very symptoms we experience when we're about to speak in public?

Take a minute right now and imagine you are about to speak in public. Really put yourself in that place: You are standing on a stage. Hot lights beam down on you, and hundreds of people are shuffling around and waiting for you to open your mouth and dazzle them with your brilliance.

What is going through your mind? How do you feel?

Many people report their breathing becomes shallow. Their palms sweat. They hyperventilate, and their hearts pound in their ears. See? When we are in fight or flight mode and when we are nervous about speaking in public, we exhibit the exact same characteristics. We will get into why that happens later, but for right now, let's talk about what goes on inside us. In fight or flight mode, what happens to our thought processes and to our actions and reactions?

The internal processes we go through in fight or flight are taking in all sorts of sensory information. That's why we might look around wildly. That frantic "Look everywhere at once" action lets us take in as much data as possible, so that we can identify the danger. But our thoughts? Our thoughts tend to run to things like "What do I need to do? Where is the danger coming from? Am I safe?" And that's the big question, isn't it? **Am I safe?**

Now, in a dangerous situation, when we're actually facing hazards, it makes sense that our amygdala, the part of our brain that controls the fight or flight response, tries to sense danger. Our more intellectual side takes the data, deliberates on it, and then decides whether or not the danger is real. Then, it determines how to respond.

On the other hand, in a situation where we're about to speak in public, are we in danger? The last time you had to speak in public, were you in danger? Were you facing actual danger or was it perceived danger? If so, what kind? What was actually causing the feeling of nervousness? Were you somehow unsafe? Were you about to die? Were you about to be hurt? Well, likely not physically. But emotionally? That's certainly possible. Our emotions are right below the surface when we speak in public, and they are easily bruised if we aren't prepared for the process.

One of the reasons our emotions are so close to the surface is that in order to be an effective communicator, we have to establish a true, authentic connection to our audience. And as soon as our feelings are in play, we all exist in a more fragile state. The most fragile, of course, is the person who has the courage to stand up and communicate authentically with others.

When you speak in public, you are the instrument. Further, you are playing your own composition. In fact, you are premiering it. Imagine you are Mozart or Beethoven: You have just written a concerto no one has heard before, and you're standing in front of a sold-out crowd. Some of them are your champions, even though you were the one chosen to premiere your composition. Many are here to listen to your wisdom. And you stand in front of them, ready to premiere this particular bit of your soul.

Is it any wonder some find this terrifying?

What are some other dangers that might cause a fight-or-flight response? We could be in the middle of a battlefield. We could be facing an armed attacker. We could be caught in a natural disaster like a hurricane. Any of those dangers would be catastrophic, and we would have every right to be terrified, not just afraid. And yet curiously, many people report the exact same reaction when they think about getting up in front of other people and speaking. Isn't that just amazing? The next part might be hard to read, but bear with me. I have a point.

The Causes of Fear.

What **exactly** is the worst that could happen if we stand up and talk to people? What might we lose? Will the sun blow up? Will a monsoon hit the building?

If we compare the risks of public speaking to potential life-ending dangers, we can gain some perspective on this. Mind you, I'm not saying that your fears aren't real, and I'm not downplaying them. What I want to do is help you get a realistic perspective on what is happening inside yourself in those moments. What makes so many people terrified of putting it out there and having their say?

If you are speaking in front of others, you might feel like you're on trial, or at least being scrutinized to within an inch of your life. But you know what? You aren't. Everyone has their own fears, thoughts, and feelings, and rarely are they about **you**. Even if someone has critical or negative things to say, their comments often reveal more about them than about you.

Certainly, we can all improve our communication skills. I am a lifelong student of perception, communication, and presentation, and I still have a ton to learn. I believe I will be gaining insights until my dying day. But what anyone else believes about you and your skills can permeate only as far as you let it. Take the best. Leave the rest. Let it become compost for another day.

We could also think of that fear as a fear of not being seen. We could see it as the fear of derision or the terror that someone else gets to judge us – and not just what we say, but who we are. We feel dozens or hundreds of eyes on us, and we desperately wish to crawl into the nearest hole and disappear. That situation strikes at something deep, something primal within us. It sparks our survival instinct. But that instinct to get away, to survive at all cost is not a conscious, intellectual response – it's a reaction to fear. And it is hard to placate with anything less than running away.

But what if we look at it another way? If we can get past that defense mechanism, if we can allay those fears, we can use that primal reaction to connect with everyone listening to us, because here's the thing: We all know that fear to varying degrees. And if we all know it, we can all connect on that plane. If we can connect on that plane and accept that everyone else has felt some version of that fear before, then we know we're going through something we have all felt. Then, we can all relax and know we are on the same page on that in-depth, primal level, and we can move and grow through it to achieve connection and partnership with one another.

And yes, since I know you're asking – I've been there too.

I feel a strange sort of kinship with people who mispronounce words that they have clearly only seen written but never heard spoken before. For example, I just heard venture capitalist Chris Sacca interviewed on the Tim Ferriss show (https://tim.blog/2017/10/05/investing-wisdom/ starting at 29:54). And he pronounced the word amalgam as "AM-ull-GAMM."

I gave him a long-distance high-five, because I've done the exact same thing many times. The first time, I was eight years old. Mrs. Saperstein, my third-grade teacher, asked me to read an SRA (Scholastic Reading Aptitude story) aloud to the class. English was still pretty new to me, since I am an immigrant, but I was able to speak it pretty well. So, I was game. I held the glossy piece of paper with the light blue border and I read a short story about a hamlet in Switzerland in front of the class. As I read, I came upon the word "picturesque," which I'd never seen before, much less heard, so I rendered that sentence as, "nestled among the snowy hills, the hamlet was picture-SKEW." (I knew the word "pictures" and I assumed "que" was pronounced like the letter q, which makes sense when you think about it.)

The class erupted. I was mortified but didn't know why until the teacher explained – and ever since then, I celebrate these little moments of bravery. Sure, you might not know the word – or have ever heard it – but if you're daring, you plow ahead and either get it right or learn something.

That moment left me terrified of speaking in public for years, but with time and perseverance I overcame my fear.

(Just so you know: You don't have to pin your fear on one big precipitating event. It could be something – or a series of somethings – else, or you might just have an introverted or shy personality. There could be any number of reasons at the root of that fear. The key, I believe, is not to judge yourself for it.)

So, we can take our bad experiences as harsh lessons that leave us too scared to speak up – like I did. Or we can change the narrative and use it as compost to grow something better. We can take a situation like mine and transform it into a victory. I didn't realize that I could change the story in my head until years later, by the way – is it possible that those of you reading this can see that you can change your story too? I believe it is, and I believe you can. We all can! So, how do we do it?

If you're one of the people who can trace your fear back to one precipitating event, I encourage you to go back and face it. Take a minute and remember that moment. Flesh it out for yourself. However, don't go back as you – go back as an observer, like a fly on the wall, and review what happened. What made you feel this fear? Did someone laugh at you? Did someone insult you or bruise your feelings? Once you have it firmly in your mind, ask yourself if there was any good information for you at that moment? Were the people involved perhaps only acting out because they, too, were afraid? Was there a different set of factors contributing to their treatment of you? It's possible they were acting out their own fear and pain, and unfortunately, your feelings got caught in the crossfire.

Take the time to forgive them and forgive yourself for your reaction. Perhaps, we can all see the universality of pain around feeling like we deserve and have the right to express ourselves. Better still, we can forgive ourselves and each other. I encourage you to do it.

If you do, then you can take that moment – and moments like it – and transform it into a challenge you can meet. The more each of us chooses to treat that unhappy moment like a learning experience, the more we will be able to connect with others, because we all know how it feels to be wrong in public, like I was when I pronounced the "que" in "picturesque."

As I think about it, I realize it wasn't just that moment. I had other reasons to be afraid, too. My father physically, psychologically, and emotionally abused my sisters and me. He beat us for the most inane reasons. Once, it happened because I didn't want to sit in a chair my father had commanded I sit on. On another occasion, instead of straight A's on my report card, I brought home five As and one A-. And on top of the abuse, we had to keep our mouths shut – we couldn't tell anyone what was happening, for fear of further violence. This was the 1970s, and there weren't the resources we have today; when the police came to our house, all they did was tell us to keep it down. They never offered us any help beyond telling my father he needed to control his temper.

I'm sure you know how well that worked. But what it did do was teach me to become as inconspicuous as possible, to keep my mouth shut and to protect my sisters as best I could.

One of his tactics still haunts me. He would hold a piece of white paper in front of us.

"I am your father," he would say. "If I say this piece of paper is black, you say, 'Yes, Dad. It's black.'"

As you might imagine, my father's abuse damaged my ability to express myself. However, it never deadened my *desire* to speak my truth. Even if I couldn't say it to him, I found other ways to say it. I sang it. I spoke it on stage. I found ways to speak truth to power. I lucked into some great teachers who helped me break out of my shell. Not everyone has that outside support, so many of us shut up and shut down, close up, and stay that way.

In the 90s, I volunteered with the Clothesline Project. Much like the AIDS Quilt, this project was started in 1990 to shed light on violence against women. Women who had survived violence made and decorated shirts with their stories. Others made shirts for women who didn't survive. At one point, we brought the Clothesline Project to the National Mall in Washington D.C., and as one of the organizers, I spoke at the exhibit.

I told my story of the piece of white paper. I told everyone about how my father used to threaten our lives if we didn't agree with him that the white paper was black.

As a child, I saved my own life when I said the paper was black. As an adult, I saved my spirit when I stood on the Mall, in front of hundreds of people and screamed, "Dad. That piece of paper was white!"

I hadn't needed to say it to his face, but I did need to say it. I needed to take that power from him and hold it in my own hands. And I did!

That moment freed me. And I believe you can free yourself, too.

But what if you're not ready for a big psychological breakthrough right now? That's perfectly fine. Let's explore some practical tools you can use if you know you have to speak in front of people and you're just terrified. (Bearing in mind that some of us have social anxiety that debilitates us to the point where we need medication or counseling – so if that's something you have a deep issue with, I encourage you to take care of yourself in the manner that works best for you.)

In my mind, that fear, that abject terror, comes upon us because of one of two things: Either we feel like we are going to totally screw it up and look like complete idiots, or we feel judged before we even go out there to speak. Regardless, it is a fear response, and the best way to deal with those responses, I think, is to name them. You could name your fear response something like Murgatroyd. Or Aloysius. Or Gertrude. But do name it. Become friends with it. Go have a beer with it.

Okay, I don't mean to go actually have a beer. But you might want to sit down and ask yourself some questions. Or rather, ask Aloysius or Murgatroyd or Gertrude some questions: Where have they come from? What is the worst that they think could happen? And really, listen to yourself for the answer, because that call is coming from inside the house. If you ask, you will find the reason why you're so terrified. And once you find it, you can deal with it.

Mission: Ask Your Fear Some Questions

Take a piece of paper. At the top half, draw your fear. Draw Murgatroyd or Aloysius or Gertrude, whichever name you chose. Is it in human form? Is it an amorphous, inky blob? What does it look like? Flesh it out and conceptualize it. That will enable you to get a handle on it. The unknown – or what we think is unknowable – always feels more dangerous than the known.

When I'm in a quandary, one of the things I'll do is think about my role. Who am I in this scenario? What am I here to do? This question, "What's my role?" is a particularly important one. It deserves its own chapter (see Chapter 12). Heck, it might deserve its own book, but we'll hit the highlights here.

Sometimes, in order to function, we need to have rules. We need to set up boundaries. We need to make our own playing field. It's impossible to play basketball without a court and some nets – if you try, you're just playing catch. You need some parameters, some tasks, a role to play. I would argue the same could be said for just about anything.

Can you make art without materials? I suppose you can sing, or dance. But even then, aren't you bound by gravity? Aren't you bound by the limits of what our bodies can do? Don't your limbs, flexibility, and strength limit you? Those are all parameters. The materials we use to make art – the pencils or paint or crayons, the paper, and the clay – they all provide a sort of boundary by giving us the medium in which we will work. Once we know that, we can start imagining how things might go.

You won't – or rather you probably won't – try to make a sculpture out of a paintbrush, some tubes of paint, and canvas. You might decide to make a still life. But will it be a sculpture? The paint tube's role is not to be a sculpture. The paint tube's role is usually to provide the color for a painting. Certainly, some artists might use it in different ways. But for the most part, we're going to use paint the way it was intended to be used. We're going to use a basketball for its intended purpose, as well. Once we know the thing's role, we know at least something about how to proceed.

I also ask myself, "If I were someone who knew how to deal with this, what would I do?" That one is a goldmine. I've used it to get myself out of the weirdest situations, and that's because it works. It works because it lets you get out of your own way. You will do for other people things you will never do for yourself – you will take chances for others, you will strive to help others, you will move mountains for them. But you will leave yourself hanging.

Often, we are warriors and heroes on the behalf of anyone else. And we won't do the same for ourselves. And this prompts the question: If you'll do it for others, what keeps you from doing it for yourself?

So, the next time you have to step in front of people to speak, or you're speaking one-on-one to someone who makes you nervous, ask yourself this question: "If I were someone who knew what to say and how to behave, what would I do?" Give yourself a few minutes to think of the answer. It will come. It's a simple exercise, but it's effective. It will surprise you.

Are Your Insides Serving You?

I heard something a long time ago that resonated with me. The very things that helped you survive when you were a child are the things that can be your biggest stumbling blocks as an adult. You developed skills in order to get by when you were a child. We all did. But those skills cost. They might make you less than flexible in some situations because those skills are born of the need to defend yourself against one thing or another. They were coping mechanisms when you were young. But they are either crutches or limiting factors for you as an adult.

Allow me to give another example from my own life.

When I was a child, in order to keep my father from getting violent, I had to convince him that he would be wrong to go forward with his plan of beating us. In his mind, we had committed some infraction that necessitated discipline. It was my job to convince him not to do it by any means necessary, so I developed incredible debate skills. I could out-argue anyone. I also had to see things in black and white: I was right, and he was wrong, and there was zero gray area. I would defend my stances vigorously because if I failed, someone would be hurt. I was a terrific debater, and no one could beat me in a discussion.

As an adult, these skills became less necessary. Yet, I kept them as my primary mode of interaction. This sort of "black and white" thinking created challenges when I needed to compromise. In fact, it made compromise a grievous error instead of a situation where everyone could get something they wanted even if they didn't win everything.

In my mind, compromise was a defeat, and defeat was dangerous. It took me years and a patient husband to stop relying solely on my debating skills to communicate. I had to build an entirely new skill-set in order to see the gray areas and learn how to give and take in discussions.

We all develop compensatory strategies as we grow up and mature. As children, we are sponges, and we learn to adapt quickly to our environment. Certainly, your strategies would not necessarily need to be as extreme as mine, but likely, you developed coping skills as you grew up as well.

Another example might be the class clown. Certainly, a child who needs attention or who wants to deal with feeling awkward or shy might become the school jokester. That skill, the ability to make a joke out of any situation is a terrific strategy for an introverted and intelligent child who needs a coping mechanism. Yet, as an adult, that same person might have difficulties being serious when a situation warrants it. They might have to overcome that inclination to make jokes in order to proceed past that awkward phase of a relationship and deepen it into intimacy.

So, we can see that those useful childhood skills might not stand us in good stead when we grow up. In fact, they might become obstacles to navigate as we move through our lives. They might even become patterns we have to dismantle in order to thrive. Take a moment and think of something that you used to do when you were a child and you faced fear or difficulties. Did you compensate? If so, what did you do? Do you still do it today? And do you ever hear from anyone that that trait or habit makes it harder to interact with you? Those skills and strategies were crucial when you needed them. But they may no longer serve you, and you will have to let them go.

Think of these skills as the stiff muscles around an injury – think of the way the muscles and tendons around a sprain often hurt worse than the sprain itself. The body sends immobilizing fluids and material to the location of an injury, because keeping it still will help it heal. After a while it heals, but the stiffness persists. And then you have to do the physical therapy to release all of that protective tissue. It had its purpose, but to regain mobility and to thrive again, you have to let it go and you have to make it dissolve. The same holds true with storytelling and communication.

An Opportunity To Share

What if we were to look at public speaking as an opportunity to connect? What if we transformed this interaction (because that is what it is) into an opportunity to share information that our audience wants and needs to have? What if our offering will give them wondrous new information, data, or entertainment that they desire and deserve? That's possible. And how would we know they want it? Because we can listen to them before we speak and get that information directly from them.

When we speak to other people, we are sharing, but we must also aim to connect. That is the end goal – connection. Even if we are nervous, we can evolve to a place where we replace the nervousness with confidence and caring. First, though, we have to check in with ourselves. We must consciously connect to our inner selves and address any fear or anxiety we have about communicating. Here are some ideas on how to check in.

I'm going to ask you to do some positive self-talk before you say anything else to anyone else. Whether you are at home, work, or out and about, head over to the nearest bathroom or place where you can be alone. Take a moment and breathe. Breathe in and out three times and then talk to yourself. I realize you will feel silly, and if you giggle, so much the better – try to go for it in the spirit of fun, and say this, or something like it:

"Self? I want to talk with you. I am here to remind you that what you are about to say is important and cool. And the people you're going to say it to will benefit from hearing you. You are going to take the time to connect with them and give them a gift, the gift of your knowledge and wisdom that they want to hear. You will truly communicate, and that is a generous and terrific thing to do."

OK, OK. That might be a little long and hard to remember. So, how about, instead, you say to yourself, "Self: Remember, you will connect, communicate, and share, and they're going to love it!"

Say it to yourself. Try it. Come on. What do you have to lose, besides your nervousness? And what you'll gain is a sure-fire technique that'll improve your ability to stand up in front of an audience with confidence and joy. Here's the thing: You won't merely improve your public speaking, because this same technique applies to any connection, communication, or conversation.

In fact, try it before your next one-on-one conversation. Take a second and connect with the other person. Listen to them. Note their speech and body language. Are they relaxed and chill or frantic and anxious? Are they happy? Sad? Contented? Rushed? See if you can glean that information before you say a word. If you are having trouble with that, it's ok. I detail more about how to observe the people you are connecting with later in the book. In the meantime, try your best to connect and communicate. You might think you're headed for failure before you even start, but nothing could be further from the truth. You will not fail. Instead, you will blow their minds.

3 DOES ANYBODY HEAR ME?

Do you know that old philosophical question, "If a tree falls in the forest and no one is around to hear it, does it make a sound?" For a long time, I tried to figure out the physics of sound waves and what happens to those physical vibrations if no instrument (microphone or ear) is there to receive them. And then I realized that none of it matters. It does not matter whether or not the tree makes a sound. The sound exists, certainly, but it gets its meaning from those who hear it. Only then does it become relevant. So, if we are going to communicate, we must all accept our right to do so. We must all learn how to do so. Then, we must all get with the program and share our victories, tragedies, wins, losses, and lives. My role in all this? It's to help you get there.

I was born to help others learn these secrets of communication that aren't really secrets. I integrated my knowledge of my role with my experience when I first began teaching groups how to sing. My first group singing class took place in the autumn of 2001, literally the week following 9/11.

See, that's what I learned when I first taught my Learn to Sing Class right after 9/11: We heal when we communicate.

We can most be ourselves when we share our stories with each other. We can most show kindness, compassion, and empathy when we listen to other people's stories. Whether they come as songs, writing, or spoken word, our stories inform, enhance, and heal us all. That first evening of the class, we spent putting our emotions into song. We breathed together. We sang, and we shared our pain and disbelief that something like this could happen. People wept and grew and healed with this experience. And I was honored to be part of helping my students (all adults by the way) communicate with song and word and heart.

It works with a song, and it works with a story. Remember that, please. The two aren't all that different because they come from and go to the same place.

After many years of doing this work, I've realized the key to success is trusting your inner guide and its connection to everyone and everything else. If you speak from that place, you will speak truths that everyone has thought or pondered – and those truths connect us to one another.

We all need and want only a few basic things; we just have wildly different ideas on what they mean and how we might attain them. Let's discuss a few of these needs and desires.

We want to feel loved. We want to feel safe. And we want to feel valued. The path we take to get there might differ from one to the next, but the overall goals are the same. So, when you speak, if you speak to those goals (in other words, put your message in the speech and/or relate it to those goals) then people will listen and they will attend to you. Once you have their attention, you are golden. But how will you know?

That last question is a trick one. You know can't truly know the answer until you first listen to your audience. Regardless of who they are and how many of them you face, first you have to listen. You have to let them know you value them, not just their opinions, thoughts, ideas, or even dollars, but them.

To step back even further, before you can let them know you value them, you have to open your heart, soul, and consciousness to knowing and valuing them without wanting or needing anything in return.

I get it. It sounds like I've swallowed some sort of bizarre happy pill. I haven't. I have discovered the secret to being a good communicator. Do you want to know what it is? Are you ready? Here goes.

To be a great communicator, you have to care, listen, and value other people. You have to be curious about who they are. Additionally, you have to discover more about them than what they say or what you see. You must delve deeper. You have to build and flex your intuition muscles and get to know the real them. You can't leave anything on the surface. You must dive deep.

You must, in essence, listen with your heart and then respond based on what you've heard and intuited. It's a reversal of sorts, isn't it? In order for them to listen and hear you, first you need to listen to and hear them. That is how we build connection, and from that place of contact, we communicate. It starts with listening and intuition. We all have the capacity for both, but we must practice in order to improve our skills. And that means we must get out of our own heads. We must put our own thoughts on the back burner so we can perceive what's going on with others.

We have all these whirling thoughts. For some, it's a constant barrage of negativity. For others, it's just a constant barrage, a never-ending storm of thoughts or ideas. We keep most of them hidden. Can you imagine what would happen if we all shared every thought that came to us? It would be chaos. No one would ever get anything done again. We would implode from all the data coming in and going – so we keep the vast majority of that marathon monologue inside.

Some of us do express our thoughts and ideas through art or writing. Some do it in other, less constructive, ways. And at least some remain convinced that no one else could possibly understand the thought storm raging inside. But I promise you this: Whatever strange, bizarre, painful, magical, miraculous monologue you have going, you are not alone. Certainly, your monologue is different from mine or from the person next to you or across the street from you. But don't for one second think that we haven't all had thoughts that surprise, shock, and scare us. We've all had them, and we'll all keep having them.

And if we all think these constant thoughts and most of us rarely express them, isn't it incredible when someone really wants to know? How amazing it must be to know that someone wants to step out of their personal pool of thoughts and see what yours is like. That's why it feels magical when we run into someone who's curious about us, or who just seems to "get" us. Think back on the last time that happened. Didn't you just want to hang out with that person? Wasn't there something magnetic about them? While I don't want to take away from that person's intrinsic value, I will say that at least some of what you found so fascinating was likely that **they** got **you**.

Earlier today, I had a serendipitous experience that illustrates this point. I was sitting in Bryant Park (near the New York Public Library) having lunch, and I spotted two men trying to find a table. When they couldn't, I invited them to join me. We found a lot to talk about, from the fact that one of them was from the former Soviet Union (like I am), to the fact that his last name is the as my ex-brother's-in-law last name (and his son's name is exactly my nephew's name), to introversion and how we can get past it, to data mining to chess and much more. It was an amazing moment for all three of us.

After a few minutes, one of them – Brian (not his real name) – asked what I do. "I teach people how to become better communicators," I answered. "Particularly if they are shy or introverted, I help them build the skills and confidence to become part of the conversation."

"Oh, wow, well actually, I'm kind of introverted. I have some trouble speaking in public," he said. "What might I be able to do about that?"

I talked to Brian about how much knowing his role would help (for a detailed discussion on knowing your role, please see Chapter 12). "For example, you are a natural problem-solver. As soon as there's an issue, you want to figure out how to resolve it and make everything better," I said.

"How do you know that?" he asked.

I'd heard them speaking about wanting a table a little while earlier, and Brian had immediately tried to solve the problem. "Well, we'll watch and see what will happen," he said. "Someone will leave, and we'll be able to grab a table."

"I heard you speaking," I answered. "I could tell immediately that you are an optimist and a problem-solver. Can you imagine how wonderful those qualities would be if you exhibited them when you connect and communicate with people?"

"That's incredible that you figured that out just by overhearing a small part of our conversation," he said. "I'm amazed that you intuited all of that."

"See, and that's the thing," I replied. "It's something we can all learn." Brian was surprised and delighted that someone got him, and that brought us closer together. It allowed for our communication to be more honest, more authentic, and frankly, more enjoyable. We didn't have to stick to safe topics. We got the opportunity to engage on a deeper and more profound level because he felt more at ease.

Another way to build that communication/listening bridge is to help people solve a problem. The rest of my interaction with these gentlemen highlights this point well.

"But what about my son?" the other man, Maxim, said. "I am not a good speaker and neither is he. He is shy, and I want him to be better able to speak and present. We've had him in a theatre improv class for years and it's not really working. What can we do to help him?"

If we want to improve our communication skills, we must remember that every person has their own path. And shy and outgoing people have different roads altogether.

"If your son is shy or introverted, you might have to find a different path for him to break out of his shell," I said. "If I were trying to help him open up and become a better communicator, I'd first want to determine what he wants to talk about. So, I'd ask him. I would find out what he likes to talk about and get him talking about it. Let's say it's chess. For this example, he loves chess. Ask him about it. Get him to talk about it to you. Ask him to explain the game and the rules. Play with him. Engage with him on the level of what he already loves, and he will want to discuss it with you. Let that be the gateway to get him communicating. He will build those skills and then as he gains confidence and desire to speak to others about his passion, you can add other topics and other ideas. Because he will have already built the skills, it will be easier for him to make progress."

The opportunity to help Brian and let Maxim know I had really seen them made it far easier to communicate with them. Given the choice, I prefer meaningful conversations to small talk. I want to delve deeply into who people are, what they think, and how they live. The more we cultivate that curiosity, the easier it will be to forge relationships that allow and encourage authentic and engaging communication.

If you want to build your speaking skills, first build your intuition and empathy skills. Become a student of the human experience. Listen to people, hear what they say, and be curious. Learn about who they are and what they really want. See how they relate to and view the world. And once you know that, meet them where they are.

Build up your intuitive powers so that you can know people. If they feel you know them and get them, you'll seem more familiar to them. If you do this authentically, you will also be more trustworthy, and a trustworthy listener is a gift we all want to receive.

Listen to how they speak. We all want to be heard. We all want to feel like people hear us. A person who authentically wants to know our thoughts and ideas becomes a revelation. So, even as you talk, make sure you keep listening. Listen to them with just as much – if not more – attention than you want them to pay to you. Give more than they do. Listen harder. Perceive everything you can from every person. These are the keys to gaining an engaged and excited audience.

Remember, listening with your ears is not enough. Open your intuition. Trust your gut and your heart when you speak to new people, and more importantly, when you spend time listening to them. Pay attention not just with your ears and eyes but with your belly. Notice your own responses to what they say and how they say it. Do you feel any tightening in your own body, perhaps your belly or the space between your eyebrows? Is there a tingling along your scalp or the back of your neck? If any sort of stray thoughts crop up as you listen and speak, pay close attention. That unbidden idea or image is chock full of data you need to know. You're getting information that can help you succeed in establishing a true, engaged, and authentic relationship.

If that information is about the people you're speaking to, evaluate it and use it to modify on the fly. (You will need to know your material well enough to do that – which we'll discuss more in Chapter 18). If the light bulb that goes on has nothing to do with what is happening, then you're losing your audience, and you need to get back in the moment. Because if you aren't excited enough to stay on your topic, you can't expect your audience to do it either. So, in addition to paying attention to them, give yourself some thought. Self-evaluate and note your own reactions to what is happening, on a mental, emotional, and physical level.

Build your awareness of yourself in relation to your audience. Are you excited, committed, and in the present moment? Do you feel a connection and electricity between you and your listeners? If the energy is there and palpable, chances are you are on the right track. If things feel grayed-out and muted, you'll need to do something to reinvigorate yourself and the audience. If you don't, you'll lose them, and your message will be lost as well.

I understand that sensing the energy in the room might be a challenge if you don't know how to do it. However, it's not a mysterious, metaphysical gift. Rather, it's a skill you can learn.

First, cultivate your curiosity about people. Before you step on any sort of stage to speak, pay attention to everyone. If you are on a bus, in a coffee shop, or any place where people congregate, speak to them. Ask questions. Get to know them. Get curious about who they are and what makes them tick.

Once you become accustomed to asking questions, take a step back. Choose a person in the room and see if you can discern who they are before you get to know them. Create their story in your head. Imagine their career, their likes and dislikes, their hobbies, and history. And then, ask. Pay attention and compare the story you spun out to their own truth. The more you do this, the more you will hone your perceptive and intuitive skills. If you build these skills and you cultivate an authentic curiosity about people, you will draw them to you. It's amazing how often someone who listens is called a great conversationalist, and someone who is authentically interested in the other person's story gets a reputation as an amazing communicator.

Bring that new awareness into your presentations. Use these intuitive skills to aid you as you communicate. You will create and nurture an energy that sparkles and draws people to you and to your message. Use this perception skill when you are presenting to foster your connection with your audience, and keep evaluating in the moment to make sure they are with you.

On the physical practical level, pay attention to body cues. If they are interested, you will know. Are they checking their phones? Are they looking anywhere but at you? If you see that, then take a second, breathe, and regroup. Refocus your message on some of those goals I just mentioned, and you will get them right back. Also, never underestimate the power of a good surprise. Change it up. Make it different. Figure out a way to stir the pot. And one of the best ways to stir the pot is to entice them with your voice. Be like a Greek Siren.

4 ON BEING A SIREN

Do you remember the myths of the Sirens who entranced sailors out at sea? They weren't just beautiful, remember. In fact, the sailors first succumbed to the lure of the Sirens' voices before they ever saw them in the flesh. The Sirens enraptured the sailors with their glorious voices, and we can do that too. (Not that I'm suggesting you enthrall a sailor and then drag them down to a watery grave or anything – just that you, too, can engage your listeners with only the sound of your voice.)

Your voice, your body language, and your energetic presence play a role in communicating your message. The words themselves can even take a back seat, because the more effectively you use your voice when you present, the more easily you will capture your audience's attention. How fabulous is that!

As we develop our spoken voice, there are a few issues to think about. Whether you are about to reach out to a live audience or doing a pre-recorded podcast or interview, here are some questions to ask yourself before you engage on a physical/sense level.

First, are you warmed up to speak? Just like a marathon runner wouldn't dream of running a race without a warmup, a speaker of any sort shouldn't present without first doing the same. Ideally, you want your mind and body prepared for whatever you ask of them. To warm up, run through the exercises in this video: https://youtu.be/zg7tjwnliig. (Copy the link or go to http://IzoldaT.com/speak-book and see Chapter 4.) It will loosen your breath, body, and vocal mechanism so you are ready to communicate. If you don't have access to the video, complete the following exercises.

But first, be aware of your abilities today. If you feel any sense of discomfort while attempting any of these exercises, please use common sense and stop. Pull back and do only what you can. If you practice these exercises, chances are you will increase your flexibility, balance, and strength – but remember to take care of yourself.

Ready to begin?

The Warmup

March in place.

After about thirty seconds, begin to slow down. Feel your feet lift off the floor. When you lift off, lift the heel first, then the ball of your foot and then your toes. Then, put your foot down with the toes first, then the ball and then the heel. Slow your steps down and sense the way your feet are standing on the floor.

Separate your feet hip-width apart; you can find hip-width by running an imaginary line up from the second toe through the center of the ankle, the center of the knees to the hip points. Take a good stance and don't lock your knees.

Roll your shoulders back and stand centered.

Lower your head and elongate the back of your neck as if you are trying to see your bellybutton.

Hold that stretch for a few seconds.

Then, bring your head up through the center and look up. Don't scrunch the back of your neck. Rather, elongate the front of your throat.

And now come back to center, bring your right ear to the

right shoulder and pull down with your left arm. Come back through center, bring your left ear to the left shoulder and pull down with the right arm.

Make sure you keep breathing deeply and fully as you do this warmup.

Come back to center and interlace your fingers behind you. Push down and back to open up the chest and to deepen your breath further.

Give yourself a big hug and look down. Breathe into your upper back so you can feel the expansion as you inhale and exhale.

Release your arms. Use the tips of your fingers to lightly pat the top of your head.

Rub your forehead, your eyebrows, and jaw hinge. Next, rub your cheeks, sinuses, nose, lips, and chin.

Make a small face (scrunch your features in) and then a large face (open mouth, eyes, and nostrils wide) and repeat that three times.

Put your hands on your belly, take a deep breath into your hands and exhale. Feel your belly expand when you inhale and contract when you exhale. Breathe like this four times.

After the fourth time, as you inhale, put your lips together and blow out through them to make "the horse noise." Inhale again and put your lips together to make the horse noise one more time.

Next time, inhale and vocalize as you blow out through your lips to make "the motorboat noise."

This is how you get the breath and the voice working together.

Now, release your arms and inhale deeply. As you exhale, open your mouth wide and yawn. Do that twice more, and enjoy the satisfaction of a good yawn.

Last, let's warm up your lips, teeth, tongue and, entire mouth. To do that, we're going to do tongue twisters. Say each one of the following tongue twisters ten times as quickly as you can. The first is "minimal animal."

The next one is "red leather yellow leather." Say it ten times as quickly as possible. Now, let's try "unique New York." After that, do "kinky cookie." The last tongue twister in the warmup is "rubber baby buggy bumper." As you get more facile with the tongue twisters, speed them up.

At this point, you should feel awake and ready. Use this warmup anytime you need to speak in front of people, and if you want a refresher on how to breathe into your belly, please see that video here https://youtu.be/gotwRRy7KBE. (You can access all of the supplemental videos at https://IzoldaT.com/Speak-book/.) And remember – if you do this warmup, you will feel more free, more confident, and more primed to shine.

Once you have warmed up, practice saying something you know well – maybe the lyrics to a song, or a favorite nursery rhyme or poem. Listen to yourself as you speak, and ask yourself the following questions: Am I loud enough? Am I too loud? How jittery, breathy or shaky is my voice? If my voice is shaky or breathy, what does that communicate? If I speak quickly, what am I saying? Can they catch all my words? Can I catch the words myself? If I speak slowly, what message am I sending? Do I know? Asking these questions – and addressing the issues that come up – will help you communicate efficiently and credibly.

Additionally, if you are speaking to a live audience, you can gauge their level of engagement and attention – but if you are recording a podcast or a video where no live audience is present, you must prepare your voice, body language, and energy level to communicate your message optimally to an audience whose reaction you cannot gauge unless they give you specific feedback afterwards.

Know Your Audience

It's good to think about how you want to communicate your message and how you want your audience to receive it. But first, you must know your audience. If you are about to present to a group of teens who spend a ton of time playing loud video games, then you can present quickly and energetically. If your audience is mostly older people, you will likely want to keep things more measured than the speaking style that would engage a fourteen-year-old. These are extreme examples, but I want to convey the importance of doing that research beforehand.

In addition to knowing the physical and socio-economic characteristics of your audience, you can delve deeper to really customize your message. Particularly if you are about to meet and communicate with a smaller group, you can learn about them as individuals. You can discover their likes and their dislikes. You can pepper what you say with what they love – it's a seasoning of a sort (yes, you see what I did there), adding flavor to your interaction with your listeners.

Let me give you an example. Back in the dawn of time, before the advent of the Internet and even before cell phones, really, I used to work for a company called The Information Prospector. The company did public records research on wealthy individuals for non-profit organizations, and the non-profits would then solicit philanthropic donations from these people.

However, they didn't just go in and say, "Hey, give us money." They did it by knowing who those people were and connecting with them on a deeper and more personal level – and at the time, before Google or any other search engines, we researched newspaper clippings and read biographies, and found the information that these non-profits needed to optimize their interactions with these potential donors. For example, one time, a public university hired us to help them solicit a donation from a business executive. So we did public records research report on him, and the research indicated that this guy loved this one particular sandwich from this one deli. So, at their initial meeting, the university representatives made sure to bring in a pile of that particular sandwich. He noticed the gesture and gave them something like a $20,000 donation – in part because they had made him feel at home.

The more you know about your audience, the more you can connect with them, and the more you can have a symbiotic relationship. Nowadays, you don't have to go to the Library of Congress. You can Google the people you'll be speaking to. Learn who they are and what they do for fun, because knowing what they love allows you to see through their eyes and communicate from their perspective. Do that before you ever open your mouth – go to Google, go to LinkedIn, find their Facebook pages. Do your due diligence. None of this is hidden information, it's in the public record, and it should inform how you will interact with these people, how you will communicate with them. Know who they are, and use that information to connect with them.

But – and this is a serious but – I *don't* mean that you should dig up and use the information in an inauthentic way. Be authentic. Be real. If your research turns up a subject you don't know anything about, be curious. Ask questions to get to know your audience better, and let them know you are interested in them. If you can find commonality, you can figure out a way to make your situation work.

Mirroring

Once you've done your due diligence and you're up there in front of your audience, it's time to try this mirroring technique. First, assess your audience: Who are they? Evaluate their body language. Are they fidgeting or still? Are their movements small? Hesitant? Big? Fast? If you can determine the general energy level and type of person in the room, mirror their movements and speech patterns if you can. Don't replicate and for sure don't mock, but do try to match the style of their movements and behaviors. They will feel more comfortable with you because you are behaving similarly to them, and you will have an easier time connecting with them.

But again, and I can't stress this enough: I'm not inviting you to be fake or misleading. I'm simply inviting you to match the level of motion and energy you receive from the people you're talking to. If it's just one or two people, it will be easier to mirror them. If it is a large group, I would advise you to move as comfortably as you can. Be authentic and try to connect with as many of them beforehand as you can.

Certainly, not all people will move or behave identically. However, you can get the lay of the land before you speak and try to connect with and acknowledge as many people as you can while doing so.

This achieves a twofold goal. First, it puts your audience more at ease. Second, if your audience seems relaxed, you will also breathe easier. That is a major benefit before you speak or present, because if you are nervous, it will show.

Nervousness can give you a shaky or breathy quality. Your voice will quiver, and you will seem scared even if you aren't. Luckily, there are a couple of easy steps to take to head off nervousness when you feel it coming on. First, take three deep breaths before you begin speaking. You might feel like eternity is passing, and people are looking at you like you've grown a second head, but there's nothing wrong with pausing in silence.

People want to fill silences because they feel uncomfortable. Let's ask the question: Why? Why does silence generate discomfort? I would bet many of us have no good answer.

Silence is preparatory. Silence is peaceful. Silence can be exciting and engaging. These are all good things, though many of us find silence frightening and anxiety-provoking. So take your time and breathe. Do a quick mental warmup. You and your audience will be better for it – in fact, I like to invite the audience to do a warmup with me when I come onstage to speak or perform. Often, they're off in their own worlds; they have worries or cares or stresses that might keep them from being here and now and ready to participate. Since I want maximum attention and participation, I invite them to stand and breathe with me. I also run them through a few short exercises so that we are all present and accounted for, as they say.

The All-important Opening Line

Here is a quick technique I use at the start of any presentation: I stand in front of the group, I look around the room and make sliding eye contact with as many people as I can, and then I let everything fall silent. Once we're all hushed, I wait until the silence is just beginning to verge on uncomfortable. Then, I change the energy of the room and turn it from discomfort into anticipation. I grin and shout "Are you ready?" The answer is always a resounding "Yes!"

And that's just what I want to hear!

You will want to find your own opening line, but I recommend you find something that immediately engages your audience. Imagine you are inviting them all to play a game with you, and let your enthusiasm spark their interest. Remember, if you aren't psyched about your topic, you can't expect them to be. Even if you are about to talk about the lackluster sales figures for last quarter's chartreuse-colored shoelaces or the history of Maltese toenail clippers, if you are excited about the topic, convey that excitement to your audience. And if you aren't excited, figure out a way to get excited. Find the humor in shoelaces. Put up a funny image in your PowerPoint deck. For example, if I absolutely had to give a presentation on shoelaces, I might start with an image of a pair of shoes hanging on a power line.

Have you seen those? Ever wondered where they come from and why people do that? There are so many potential answers and they range from someone playing a joke to a gang establishing its territory. However, despite what various sources say, there is no definitive answer – so, make this a way to engage your audience. Ask them if they know. Make it a guessing game. Make it funny. Offer a prize for the best answer before the end of the presentation. The prize can be a doughnut, by the way – it doesn't have to be a big item. People love contests they have a chance of winning! That doughnut will get them to think about laces in a new way, and it will improve your presentation because they'll be with you

– pretty good work for a simple doughnut.

That's part of your responsibility as a presenter. Do what you need to do to get and keep them with you. Sing a song. Tease them with a doughnut. Don't give them a chance to check out. Bring them in with your first breath, your first sentence, and they'll be with you – or at least they'll be yours to lose, rather than yours to struggle for. That is a much stronger and bolder place to be.

5 LET'S TALK "LOUD."

Before we go any further, let's explore what it means to be loud. When you speak loudly, are you being authoritative? Knowledgeable? Confident? Bullying? Obnoxious? Dynamic? Urgent? Informative? A number of scenarios come to mind when we think of someone speaking loudly or shouting. They could be warning us of danger. They could be chiding us. They could be excited and enthusiastic about sharing their excitement. They could be from New York! (Kidding. Lots of places have loud citizens. New York gets a bad rap sometimes, I think.) That sort of communication has its place, and many have used it to great effect.

Allow me to introduce another concept: If you want people to hear you, instead of just speaking louder, try projecting your voice. I'm not recommending you head off to ventriloquist school or anything like that (unless you want to, and then have at it). Rather, I am talking about engaging your voice and employing a technique that allows you to fill the space in which you are speaking. When you do so, you will also engage every single person who hears you.

Think about the singers and orators of a century and more ago. When Emile Berliner invented the carbon-button microphone in 1876, (Wired Magazine, January 11, 2011), he turned sound into a signal that could be broadcast and enhanced. Before then, singers, speakers, and orators relied on their own voices – and perhaps megaphones – to be heard above the roaring crowd. How did they do it? They projected. Projection can be challenging to master, but it's worth it. And the best part is, you can start to learn it right this second. Here's the secret no one ever tells you about vocally filling a large space: You don't have to get louder to do it. In fact, if you try to get super loud (and you think of it in those terms), you might strain your voice and end up with only a sore throat to show for your efforts.

Instead, focus on these three things. First, work on keeping your speaking voice at the same, normal volume. You don't need to strain to it to project.

Second, get into your breath. Proper breathing helps us speak more effectively and handles anxiety we might feel about speaking, so concentrate on deepening and lengthening your inhalations and exhalations.

You might be tempted to take short, shallow breaths if you are nervous. Instead, slow everything down. Breathe in for a slow count of three and breathe out for another three count. Do this three or four times. A word of caution: Many of us aren't used to breathing deeply, and when we start, we might feel dizzy or lightheaded. Take care of yourself. If you start feeling lightheaded, take a seat until the feeling passes. When you increase the flow of oxygen into your bloodstream, your body loves it but might have a bit of trouble dealing with it. So, get used to the deeper breaths before you take it out on the road, as it were.

Once you have the deeper breath going, make sure your shoulders aren't rising on your inhalations. Rather, see if you can make your belly expand on the inhale and contract on the exhale. Don't force it, but instead allow the natural expansion and contraction to occur. Here's a helpful metaphor: Imagine you are a balloon. When the balloon "inhales," it is getting filled with air. The balloon increases in size everywhere, not just the top. And in fact, the air heads down and fills the balloon up in the middle, which is just where you want to imagine the air going inside you. Imagine your middle is the inside of the balloon – it expands when you inhale and contracts when you exhale. Now, let's say you want to deflate the balloon in a controlled manner. You will pinch the opening so that the balloon doesn't deflate too quickly. When the balloon deflates, each side of the rim of the opening rubs against the other, and the vibration of the air escaping makes that high-pitched sound as it rushes past – which describes almost exactly what's happening with your own vocal chords when you make a sound and support it with your breath. The vocal chords – or folds – are responsible for the actual sound of your voice. (Most people know them as vocal chords, but they are shaped more like folds. For a more in-depth look at how the vocal apparatus works, please see this *Journal of the American Medical Association (JAMA)* article: jamanetwork.com/journals/jama/article-abstract/373747.)

Mission: Fun with Balloons

Find a balloon and blow it up. Pinch the opening almost shut with one hand. And then with the other, gently squeeze the balloon in a controlled fashion. You should hear a sound emanate from the opening of the balloon. The softer and more controlled the squeeze, the more consistent the sound that comes out. If you push too hard, the sound will shriek and end too quickly. If you push too softly or inconsistently, that, too, will impact the quality of the sound. A controlled, gentle push from the bottom of the balloon will give you the most consistent and long-lasting sound.

Practice this until you get the hang of it. And when you apply the same technique to your own breath, you'll notice a great difference in the amount of air you take in and the control you have over your breathing speed and vocal volume. You might even notice a sense of calm coming over you. Enjoy that calm. It's a beautiful thing that stems from your deepened breath.

Third, once you've mastered the balloon squeeze, there's one more thing to incorporate, so go ahead and put that balloon down. You won't need it for this next part.

As you breathe and open your mouth, choose a focal point for your voice – an object that is no more than three feet away from you. Now, breathe in, focus on the object, and speak to it without raising your voice consciously. Say whatever comes into your head, but say something. You can even try, "Hello, [name of object]!" Maintain an awareness of both your volume and the amount of effort it is taking for you to reach the object.

Keep notes on paper or make mental notes, but be sure you increase your awareness of your surroundings and your effect while you practice projection.

Once you have gotten the hang of speaking to an object three or four feet away, practice changing your focal points. Keep breathing and keep everything else the same, but try speaking to something six or eight feet away. You will notice that your voice is louder and you can "reach" the object pretty easily. Now, try it at the end of the space you're in. Afterward, try the top corner of the space farthest away from you. Take note of how your voice sounds. Is it louder? And are you working any harder to make it so? Practice this technique until you are comfortable with it – and then add one more layer. Stand at one corner of the room and engage and project to the opposite top corner. Imagine yourself filling the entire space with just your voice.

How did that go? If you want to try a bigger room or to go outside, go for it. And let me know how it goes. I'd love to hear all about it.

Mission: Move it move it

Here is another quick and simple technique to help you project. Have you ever watched a singer belting out a long note on a power ballad? If you haven't paid a lot of attention to that, go right now and find Lea Michele's fabulous version of "Don't Rain on My Parade" on YouTube (https://youtu.be/BLTYh2RM4pA). Watch and see what she does with every note that needs to be big, and pay special attention from 2:30 until the end.

When you need to project, do what Lea Michele does in that video. Use your body. Move your arms. Make your entire frame one big energetic megaphone, and you will be amazed at how much you project, without effort, and fill whatever space you need to fill.

Now, try this fun exercise. Grab your balloon again and blow it up. Then, release it. Follow it with your voice as it careens around your space. Project your voice to it and see how far it carries. Build this skill, and you will be able to project and connect with your entire audience.

6 A SCREAM TO A WHISPER

Loud voices grab our attention, but a soft voice, used properly, will keep it. When we want people to **listen** to us, rather than just hearing us, we can increase the urgency of our speech by softening it. Let's have them leaning in. Let's have them at the edge of their seats and hanging on our every word. If we vary our volume and projection, we will keep the audience excited and compelled. They won't know whether or they're coming or going – and that can be a good thing, depending on the type of presentation you are giving. Ultimately, it comes down to comfort level. If you are comfortable with loud, but soft scares you, stay loud until you get comfortable going soft, and vice versa. Just make sure you keep pushing those boundaries.

To go soft but still fill a room, you can employ a similar projection technique to the one from the previous chapter. Choose your focal point that's close by, say the same lamp you chose before, and speak to it. However, this time, instead of saying "Hello, lamp," try the following sentence.

"I've got a secret to tell you."

Now, say these words to the other focal points that you chose in chapter 5. Note any changes in the volume and urgency in your voice. The words themselves connote a sense of secrecy and urgency, so you aren't going to want to say them loudly. Instead, focus on saying them at the exact same volume, but with more urgency.

Go ahead and physicalize the telling of a secret to make it more compelling. Cup your hands around your mouth as if you were a child about to whisper to a trusted friend. Even though you might be saying the words to the far corner of your living room, the action of cupping your hands and the words themselves will lend a sense of urgency to what you're saying. If you bring your body into the act of saying the words, and use it to color what you're saying, you will make those words more compelling and exciting without having to raise your voice a bit. That's exactly how you begin to show presence.

Presence

Projection works beautifully when you need to fill a space with your voice. However, it's not always the best option when you want to fill a space with your presence. If you want to do that, you might want to leave your voice on the softer side, keeping the urgency but projecting less, so people have to lean in to hear you. If you foster a sense of mystery and urgency, you will captivate them. A soft voice, when it contains energy, can enthrall people. Soft can mean intimacy, vulnerability, and secrets. Soft can mean enticement, and that can make all the difference, depending on what you have to say.

I imagine you might be thinking, "Soft. I can do soft. Soft isn't a problem. Loud is the thing that's tough." And I would disagree, to a point. Soft by itself isn't that hard, but being soft with urgency, soft with energy – that's significantly tougher to achieve than loud.

If you want to infuse your speech patterns with that intimate quality, strive for a softer, more melodic cadence (cadence is the rhythmic flow of a sequence of sounds or words). You will need to control your breathing even more – but as a bonus, you'll get rock-hard abs if you do this for long, because the breathing techniques you need to maintain your energy levels are *challenging.*

The best way to describe it is that you must maintain a huge output but a laser focus. Your voice will be powerful, but it won't diffuse to everyone in the room all at once. Rather, you will connect with individuals. Make sure you engage with people one-on-one while you speak to them with this soft-but-focused energy. That is powerful. It will bring you a more intimate connection and help you make a more direct impact on your audience.

Think about it. In the movies, when someone needs to get your attention, they don't always yell. In fact, you've probably heard the phrase, "You know when you really have to worry? When she gets quiet." And it's true. Quiet, stillness, silence, they make us nervous. If someone is loud, we tend to think of them as a "what you see is what you get" sort of person. There's nothing hidden. You know who they are. And there's nothing wrong with a big voice or personality, but that can be a little much for some people. After all, variety is the spice of life – and variety in tone and timbre can engage an audience in different ways.

As a speaker, you have to gauge the room. If you feel like you're in a good place to speak robustly, do it. If, on the other hand, the audience wants a quieter intensity, you can employ techniques that will allow you to own the room without ever once raising your voice.

Again, this is as much about self-awareness as it is about

communication. It is also about knowing the other people involved. If you know your audience, all things are possible.

7 PITCH PERFECT?

Let's talk about pitch. First, do you know what I mean when I say pitch? Allow me to give a brief overview. Vocal pitch (the actual tones and notes in which we speak) can be high or low. And just like with soft and loud voices, we tend to ascribe meaning to voices of different pitches. Someone with a high-pitched voice comes across younger and less experienced. Why? Children tend to have shorter vocal folds (sometimes also called vocal chords). That means their voices will be pitched higher.

Mission: The Marriage of Vocal Folds and Physics

Try this experiment. Get two rubber bands, a short one and a long one. Hold the shorter one between your thumbs and pull it slightly, so that there's a bit of tension on the rubber band. Then, use one of your other fingers to strum it like it's a guitar string. Listen to the sound that comes out. Now, take the longer rubber band and repeat the procedure. Could you hear a difference in the sound between the two rubber bands?

If you did notice a difference, what was the difference?

Did the smaller rubber band sound lower or higher? What about the larger rubber band? Did it sound lower than the smaller one? It should have. That's because the longer a rubber band – or vocal fold – the lower in pitch it will be. So, when we are young, we have tiny little vocal folds, and everything we say sounds higher in pitch. As males grow, their vocal folds grow to the point where they go through a change, and their voices get significantly lower. Female voices also change as girls go through puberty, but not nearly as much as do male voices.

Additionally, as both men and women age, our vocal folds loosen. As they loosen, they lengthen. As a result, our speaking voices (and singing voices) lower as we get older.

Mission: The Daily Pitch Cycle

Have you ever noticed that when you first wake up in the morning, your voice sounds lower than it does later in the day? If you haven't, pay attention tomorrow morning. Say something, and note where you speak comfortably. I'll bet that it's significantly lower than where you'd speak the exact same thing comfortably later in the day. Record yourself with your phone first thing after you wake up, and then record yourself saying the same thing six or seven hours later. You'll note a drastic difference in the pitch of your voice between the two, because the vocal folds relax while you sleep, and the more relaxed they are, the longer they are. Consequently, their pitch will be lower when you've just woken up.

That's what I love about physics. It just keeps working.

Pitching Lessons

So, we think of high-pitched voices as coming from

younger or more inexperienced people. Does a lower-pitched sound necessarily mean more experienced? It might. Someone who has a low-pitched voice can definitely *sound* authoritative. Remember, a lower-pitched voice connotes an older person, and we can, therefore, infer that it will also connote someone with more experience and wisdom.

However, go ahead and find Barry White's famous song, "Can't Get Enough of Your Love Baby." In it, he doesn't sound as authoritative as much as he sounds like he's ready to get down and get with it. A certain amount of passion and soulful ardor is characteristic of low-pitched voices, as well.

Male versus female voices also have connotations. Think about a feminine-sounding voice. What images or thoughts does it bring up for you? What about a male voice? Listen to a few commercials with both voices in them and note how they make you feel. More to the point, take note of whether or not it's the fact that the voice is male/female or high- or low-pitched that makes the difference. While most of us can't change our voices too drastically (and I wouldn't recommend it anyway, because too big a change will also come across as inauthentic), we can control our pitch to a great extent. And we can use pitch, volume, and resonance to an amazing effect if we know how to do it. In the next section, I will introduce effective techniques to help.

First, though, I should say that this is not all about your voice. Or rather, it's not all about the vocal apparatus in your throat. The rest of your body must be part of the process. In fact, you use your entire body to speak – or what I call your energetic body. When you speak, there are sympathetic vibrations that go from below your toes to above your head. And when you modulate your voice or change your speaking pitch, those vibrations move naturally and sound in different parts of your body.

So, it isn't just your vocal folds that vibrate. If you're speaking low in your voice, other parts of your body will vibrate in harmonics with your vocal folds to generate resonance. In fact, that's what gives your voice its character, because the vocal folds vibrating by themselves is an unimpressive sound. What gives you timbre and melody is the rest of your body.

Mission: Chest voice/head voice resonance direction

Take a deep breath. Put your hand on your chest. And then in a very deep, low-pitched voice make a "Ha, Ha, Ha," sound.

Did your hand pick up any sort of vibration while you were making the sound? More importantly, did you notice that it stopped when you stopped making this sound? If you didn't feel it, play around with the pitch of your voice until you do. Once you feel it, I want you to give me a Homer Simpson "Woohoo!" And if you don't know what that is, go to YouTube or Google and type in "Homer Simpson Woohoo." There are a lot of videos (like this one: https://youtu.be/DFloZbT99oE) that demonstrate it.

Now that you know what a "Woohoo!" is, put your hand on your chest and give me one. Chances are, you didn't feel that same vibration in your chest as when you made the low "Ha, Ha, Ha," sound. There's a reason for that.

But, before I tell you what it is, I'm going to ask you to do one more thing. With one hand on your chest, do a combination of a low "Ha, Ha, Ha," and a high "Woohoo." Do it several times. What do you notice about the vibrations in your chest? Can you tell when they're there, and when they aren't anymore? It's an important distinction.

Where do you think those vibrations go when they aren't

in your chest? Do they travel around your body? Where might they go?

Mission: The Homer Simpson, "Woohoo!"

Why don't you try it? Put one hand on your chest and the other one on your nose and do that "Ha, Ha, Ha," and then the Homer Simpson "Woohoo." See where the vibrations could go, depending on which sound you're making. Put your hand on your nose, or on your sinuses, or perhaps on your forehead while you make the "Woohoo!" sound. Did you feel vibrations anywhere? I'm betting you did.

It's pretty interesting, isn't it? This is all one big way of saying that the vibrations go into different parts of our bodies depending on the pitch of our voices. And what's more, we can nudge those vibrations where we want them to go and make our sound bigger, fuller, and more resonant.

As part of this process of finding your voice, you will learn to feel where your voice is going, and how to direct it where you want it to go. You can build this skill to the point that the physical direction of your voice is second nature. Then, you'll have a full, nuanced, and resonant voice that will support your communication and make it shine. Your natural excitement for your topic will inform the way your voice moves and flows throughout the telling of your tale, and these techniques will augment your presentation.

It's important that what you feel about your topic comes through. The natural cadence of our voices affects our listeners, and a more melodic flow will help capture their attention and their imaginations. That's why, when we were children and we heard someone delightedly say "Once upon a time" with that sing-song quality, we thrilled to what they were saying.

With a monotone, the phrase and the voice lose their luster. If we love what we're talking about, we will naturally have that cadence – the hills and valleys, the ups and downs, and the flow. However, sometimes nervousness can dam up that flow. But guess what? We can still do something about it.

Regardless of how we naturally speak or perform, we can express a little extra. We can sound like ourselves – but just a little bit more.

Think of someone whose voice goes up and down a lot when they speak. What does it make you think of? Do those kinds of peaks and valleys in a voice make you think of someone who sounds lethargic or bored with their topic, excited about their topic, or neutral about their topic? What do you think? Those highs and the lows – what do they connote? Conversely, what does a relatively flat affect connote? Does it make you feel the excitement? Does it bring up a sense of danger? Or does it feel dry, verging on arid?

You see, we can build our awareness. We can learn to evaluate and judge the type of storyteller in front of us. Some storytellers will give us that excitement, verve, and magic with only their voices to do it (think of the last great audiobook you heard). Other storytellers come across more flat, perhaps more contemplative, or more thoughtful. This is not to say the speakers who modulate a lot are not thoughtful, or that flat-affect speakers are lethargic and uninterested in their own topic.

It does, however, suggest that we can build an awareness and evaluate the quality and characteristics of a speaker based on a modulated versus a flattened affect in their speech. If we open our senses, we will understand a deeper truth than just the words being said – and that is a critical skill to possess.

What's fascinating is that this kind of awareness will work in any conversation or situation – including interviews and presentations. If you are interviewing for a position, the way you present yourself vocally will give conscious and unconscious clues to your interviewers. If you are breathy or rushed, they will give thought to whether or not you are nervous or ill-prepared. If you are hesitant, you might be seen as under-prepared. If you are overly loud, they might see you as arrogant.

What you want to do is play between the lines of well-modulated, but not overly excited. Again, be authentic. Say what you mean and remember to breathe. And use these key techniques to sound your best: Sit between rushing your words and hesitating too much between them. Take a breath before you answer a question. Collect your thoughts. And then speak with energy and confidence.

Modulate your pitch and speak as quickly as feels comfortable, without painting yourself into a corner where you have spoken too quickly. If you speak too quickly, you might get to a point where you either don't know what you want to say next, or you have over-spoken and now need to correct yourself.

Remember, we all must strive to sound as natural as possible. But in any sort of live speaking situation, we need to work for what I call natural-plus.

Natural-plus isn't just an innate talent, by the way. It comes with diligence and practice. By the time we're through, you will have control over these various parts of your voice. You will be able to choose how and what you project to any audience. You will be able to soothe or inspire. You will amaze and comfort. And you will do it all with just the power of your voice.

8 NATURAL-PLUS

What do I mean by natural-plus? Do I mean you need to supplement your authentic communication patterns with something extra? Yes, I do. Of course, we want to sound natural. However, the way we speak to our friends over a beer or our spouses when we're waking up in the morning might be natural, but that's not an ideal way to speak when we are communicating with others in public.

We need to remember that when we make a presentation, we are using our voices to tell the story, and that story is not our shopping list. Our tale has a greater significance, so we must use our voices, our bodies, and our energy to convey it in a way that will inspire, enthrall, and engage our listeners. Audiences fatigue quickly. If we cannot use our bodies, minds and voices to tell the story effectively, we will lose them.

Mission: Reading with Hills and Valleys

Before we go any further, I want you to try another experiment. Go to your bookshelf and grab any book that is fiction. Open it to a random page. Read the first five sentences at the top of that page in as a flat voice as you can.

Read the book with the words coming out one every second. Try not to raise or lower your voice at all. See if you can get through all five sentences without feeling like you need to go take a nap. Are you ready? Go! Try the same sentences and infuse your voice with excitement. Evaluate your response to the reading. Better? Worse? Did you feel like napping, or was there a bit more pep in your vocal step? Think about it.

Now, go find the most exciting book on your bookshelves (make it one you have read before). Find a thrilling part of the book, turn to the page, and read it in the most significant monotone that you have ever attempted. Make it as boring as possible with your voice. Then, try it with that same excitement as before. Evaluate it.

Now, do the opposite. Find some writing that's as drab as watching paint dry, and infuse it with excitement. And give thought to your responses as the listener. Interesting, isn't it?

I don't know if you've ever heard this, but many people say that men like James Earl Jones or Benedict Cumberbatch would sound terrific reading the telephone book. They probably would. That's because they know how to use their voices. They know how to pitch them and modulate them so that when they speak, we want to keep listening. And we don't really care what they're saying.

Try this a few more times with a few more pieces of writing. Tell the story with vocal modulation and try the same story in a lackluster monotone. Then, change each one a little bit until you reach a happy medium – not too elated and not too monotone, but conveying excitement and engagement. Remember, you want it to be authentic, but you want it to be authentic plus a little bit more. See? It's natural-plus.

Your enthusiasm for your topic must convey to your audience. You achieve that authentic connection with your voice, your body, and your story.

Mission: Tell Yourself a Story

Every night before you go to sleep, pick up a book. Make it a book you love. Read it out loud, as if you were telling its story to a rapt audience that's hanging on your every word. Your story can be an epic adventure or literary fiction. It can be anything you want, but the key is you have to make it the most interesting story ever told to anyone by anyone.

At one time, storytelling was information as well as entertainment. Stories passed down tribal knowledge. They passed down history. Stories passed down details of the people, their struggles, their history, their families, and their lives.

In Native American cultures in the Southwest, there is a mythic figure called "The Storyteller." She is depicted, in sculptures and statues, surrounded by children who are listening to her tall tales and hanging on her every word. (See a storyteller image here: https://IzoldaT.com/speak-book/ under the Chapter 8 heading.) I have several of these statues in my house. They remind me of the importance of stories in our history.

Before the written word, we told our tales. Before movies or books, the oral tradition existed and thrived. Through stories, people remembered their history, made plans, and explained unknown phenomena. The changing of the seasons in ancient Greece, for example, was explained by the myth of Persephone and her mother Demeter. The rising and setting of the sun was the story of Helios the charioteer. In West African and Caribbean folklore, Anansi was the god of all tales and a major figure in many of them. Stories of such tricksters as Coyote or Raven in the Native American lands explained creation. Stories inspire us, soothe us, excite us, and fill our hearts. A single word, specifically ordered, can change destinies.

Mission: "I love you" – Modulation with Focused Intent

Take the phrase, "I love you," from the first mission. Instead of focusing just on word emphasis like you did before, bring modulation and focused intent into the equation. Write out the different ways you could say it. Could you say it with derision? Could you say it with passion? Could you say it as a question? Say it as if you were angry. Say it as if you are in love. Say it as if you are incapable of believing that you feel the depths of this feeling.

What do you have to do with your voice to say the phrase as if you feel the above feelings? What do you have to change? How do you phrase it? If you aren't feeling excitement, passion, or anger, what do you need to do to convey it anyway? Use your vocal inflection to express the feeling. Keep practicing until you can do it on command. It will help you utilize your voice in public speaking. I can't say this enough, though: I don't want you to be disingenuous when you speak in public. What I want is for you to have all the tools in your toolbox, so you can be present, authentic, and engaging when you communicate. If these techniques are second nature, you will be able to concentrate on communicating.

Try the above exercise with other phrases. Try it with the phrase, "I need you." Try it with, "Who wants this?" And when you're ready, try it with longer phrases like "What can I do for you?" See how it feels to change the emphasis and the modulation of the phrase. As you improve, you will do it with longer ones. But for now, stick with three or four-word phrases. See what it feels like to change the pitch of the phrase. The pitch, modulation, cadence, and emphasis all affect how your audience hears and responds to your message. Head over to this video for samples of these and other phrases (https://IzoldaT.com/speak-book/ under the Chapter 8 heading.)

The Monotone

Now that we've discussed modulation, let's address its opposite, the monotone. Someone who is nervous, scared, or delivering dry or repetitive data might be tempted to express it in a monotone. Factual, ordered dissemination of information can seem like the way to go.

However, nothing could be further from the truth. Even the driest and most complicated data can come at you from an exciting and compelling place when the person who delivers it knows what they're doing.

Do you remember how I said that someone like James Earl Jones could read the phone book and delight us? For those of you who might prefer a lady's voice, think Kathleen Turner in 1985, Isabella Rossellini, or even Emma Stone with that husky flavor to her voice.

If James Earl Jones can make a phone book exciting and new, why can't you do that with a recitation of your accomplishments in an interview? Or perhaps you have to deliver lackluster sales numbers figures at your company's year-end conference. You can still put your best foot forward and tell it like it is – with a bit of added spice. What you say can be spruced up and made more engaging without altering any of the facts and figures.

But for now, let's get back to the monotone. Remember, if you find yourself nervous before a presentation or any sort of speech, and you fear you'll end up droning along in a monotone, you can modify your speaking mechanics with pitch and modulation. You can also vary the speed of your words. I guarantee that if you deliver everything slowly, so that each word has the same length of time and emphasis, you will find your audience's eyes rolling back in their heads and soft snores wafting your way.

So, even if you don't feel passionate about what you're saying because you're too scared, vary your speed and pitch and you will do better than you think.

Of course, when you're modulating or varying the speed with which you speak, you want to come from an authentic place. In other words, you want your speech to be influenced by your feelings and your desire to convey something truthfully. Sometimes, we all get too scared and nervous to do it properly. Fear makes us uncertain that we deserve to be heard or that our views and thoughts have value. What are we to do then? We have to rely on the old chestnut: Fake it 'til you make it. Ideally, you would believe in your message so strongly that the vigor and passion you feel for your topic would flow out of you and envelop the audience in a haze of glorious attention.

However, if you are too nervous, that's OK. You can always rely on some of the techniques we mentioned earlier. Make eye contact with several members of the audience. Smile and engage with them energetically. Broadcast your intention and your willingness to connect and interact with them. Make them feel like you're all sitting together around a small table in an intimate, setting rather than in a cavernous auditorium.

How do you do that? You have to imagine it. Project that notion in your own mind. Flesh out what a cozy space would look and feel like to you. Imagine it and make it real in your head. And then behave like you would if you were sitting around with a bunch of good friends (not the swill-beer-and-tell-fart jokes kinds of friends, unless that's appropriate for what you're talking about, but dear friends nonetheless). If you act like you're at home, they will be too. If you make the space – regardless of its size – something intimate, fun and engaging, they will respond accordingly.

Note: Some people cannot help speaking in a monotone. They are tone deaf, physically tone deaf, and they have no capability of distinguishing one pitch from another. If this is an issue for you, there are other ways to engage an audience, and we will discuss them later.

The big thing to remember is that, as much as possible, you want to let your intuition and your natural flow guide the modulation and the speed of your speech. The more natural and authentic you sound, the more your listeners will relax into hearing what you have to say and really taking it in. Authenticity is key. You can do a pretty close facsimile, but deep down your audience will know if you're faking your truth. As much as possible, be real with them, and your truth will ring out to them.

9 RESONANCE

Let's talk about resonance. Resonance is the vibrational quality and fullness of sound that your voice has when you speak. That resonance can be thin and reedy, or it can be full with a lot of overtones. The more rich and resonant your voice sounds, the more those vibrations are moving throughout your entire vocal instrument, your body. And the more you communicate with your full being, the more you can connect with your audience on a whole and holistic level.

That's the thing no one tells you: The more you can infuse your voice into the resonating chambers in your body, the more well-rounded, resonant, and engaging you'll sound. People like Benedict Cumberbatch and James Earl Jones? Their voices resonate everywhere, and that's part of what makes them so powerful.

Vocal Resonating Chambers: The sound amplifiers of the body

So what are these resonating chambers that no one told you about? Of course, we have the actual vocal folds in what sometimes is called the voice box, or the larynx. But we also have other resonating chambers in our bodies, hollow places that help our voices produce vibrations for a richer sound. Our mouths, for example.

Mission: The Ah Sound

Try this experiment. Take a deep breath in and say, "Ah," for a count of five. Do it again, and this time pay attention to how wide open your mouth is and how far apart you are holding your teeth.

Was your mouth open wide, or did you have your teeth close together? Now, do it again. This time when you make the "Ah" for that five count, make sure that your teeth are far enough apart so that the tips of your index and middle finger, held vertically, fit between your top and bottom front teeth.

For a quick demonstration of the Two-finger Rule, go to https://IzoldaT.com/speak-book under the Chapter 9 heading.

Do the same thing one more time – only this time, have your teeth separated just as they were when you first started making the "Ah" sound. Do you notice a change in the sound you're making? If not, try it again a few more times. Pay attention to the quality of your sounds. Don't judge yourself, please, as that will make things more arduous than they need to be. Instead, just take note of the sounds you're making. We're just getting started on making your voice the best it can be. Take baby steps, and remember: Babies don't judge themselves harshly when they're learning how to walk. Every time they fall on their tushies, they simply get up and try again. If they stopped to judge themselves, we would be a world of crawlers.

Experiment with how wide you're opening your mouth, and listen for the changes in timbre (characteristics of the sound). You might notice you have a louder and fuller sound when your mouth is open a little more. Why is that? It's because you have a bigger resonating chamber when your mouth is open.

Think about a guitar. Have you ever noticed the round hole in the center of the body of the guitar? That's called the sound hole. (the image, is at https://IzoldaT.com/speak-book under the Chapter 9 heading.)

Although the vibrating strings, the guitar's version of the vocal folds, sit on the outside of the guitar, that sound hole is what truly magnifies the music and sends it out to listeners. And as long as we're thinking about musical instruments, picture the differences between a small violin and a large bass. See the two images here: (Violin and Stand-up bass images https://IzoldaT.com/speak-book). Notice that the violin has a small body that's well suited for resonating with the high notes of its short strings. A bass, on the other hand, has a much bigger body, and the notes are fuller and more resonant because of its greater size. Each is geared towards the producing the best sound for the pitches it plays. So think about the pitches you want to produce, and whether you need a violin or a bass when you open your mouth. A mouth resonating chamber of the optimal size and shape brings the best sound to our audience.

Have you ever noticed how much opera singers open their mouths when they sing those full, huge notes? While we don't have to create the same amount and quality of sound when we speak in public, we can employ similar techniques to achieve our vocal quality goals. If our voices sound more resonant and full, they're more authoritative and easier to hear. And that leads to better connection, interaction, and communication with our audience.

Sinuses and Speaking

Another way to increase your resonance is to make sure that you've cleared your sinuses before you speak. Your sinus cavity is one of your main resonating chambers, and it has a real effect on the sound of your voice. If your sinuses are stuffed up, you will have a specific sound, that stuffy, nasally sound you get when you have a cold – and you'll also lose the ability to make several of your consonants.

Mission: Consonants and a Stuffed-up Nose

Squeeze your nostrils shut with your thumb and your index finger and try to say the letter N. Does it sound a little bit more like a D? Try to say an L while you're plugging your nose. What does it sound like? Is it different than usual? I'll bet it is.

Speaking with Intent

We all have unconscious habits that we have developed over the years. These habits, like filling spaces with "um," sniffing, or clearing our throats are interruptions to the flow of thought and our ability to listen. So here's another quick tip: Blow your nose before your interview, important meeting, or presentation. You'll increase the resonance in your voice, and you won't sniff as much.

The dreaded "um" also needs to go. We all know we shouldn't do it, and the majority of us use it as a crutch. Whenever we're not sure of what we are going to say next, we default to "um," "like," or another vocal placeholder; it makes us feel safer because it takes up room and sound in our space.

Yet, just because it fills a silence doesn't mean it's a good idea. We feel like it's providing resonance, sound, and something for our listeners to hang onto while we essentially stall for time. But instead, we're putting filler out there, and that diffuses our message. Start listening for "um" in your speech; notice when you're using it. And instead of defaulting to that vocal placeholder, build a sense of comfort with the pause. Radio people say it's "dead air" when no one's speaking. But I like to think of it as breath. When you pause in silence instead of filling the room with an "um," you are leaving space for your listener(s) to breathe, much like the white space on a piece of paper leaves the reader room to think.

In that instant of silence, take a moment and reconnect with the people listening to you. Acknowledge everyone in the room as well as yourself, and make sure they all know that you are there, present, with them in that moment and for the duration of your acquaintance. The more people know your authentic regard for them, the more they will respond in kind because some part of each of us recognizes the need to be heard and understood. It's ancient and primary to our survival.

10 FOCUS AND FRAGILITY

Let's talk about what I like to think of as charisma. Some people are able to walk into a room and draw everyone else to them. They draw eyes, and they draw attention. When you are speaking to a group, no matter the size, you want to invite your listeners towards you. Draw them with your voice and energy, and one of the best ways to do that is through silence – silence and connection. Communicate with your body instead of your voice for an instant. And I know this is an oldie, but one of the best ways to do that is simply to smile – just remember, you aren't smiling out of nervousness. You are smiling to engage and (re)connect with your audience. Even if the nerves are there, don't let them lead your energy. Imagine that you've got this, and you do!

We as a society and as a people have gotten away from communication that is energy and body-oriented. We do so many things online we no longer have that entire avenue with which to connect to others. We miss eye contact, so we have a tougher time communicating – and I would even argue we are losing the ability to read and interpret body language, and therefore intent. (That, perhaps, is another entire book.)

Regardless, the way we communicate leaves a lot up to

interpretation, and the more we can see each other and interact with one another, the more we can take in and respond to silent, non-verbal cues. (See the work of Albert Mehrabian and the 7-38-55 Rule for more information on the relative importance of words, tone, and body language. http://www.kaaj.com/psych/index.html.) Email ultimately cannot take the place of a face-to-face meeting. Video platforms that allow meetings across time and distance are fabulous, because they bring back that additional set of insights, body language and eye contact – to an extent. However, these platforms don't really allow for eye contact. Have you noticed that when you use Skype, Zoom or any other video platform, you look at the screen, and that means you're looking down to the person viewing you rather than meeting their eyes? That's because the camera is up at the top center of most monitors.

The same goes for phones. Have you ever noticed how if you take a selfie but you don't look at the camera, your eyes are just a little off-center? That's because there is a little bit of difference between the center of the screen and the camera.

Mission: Phone Selfie

Go to the bathroom mirror and bring your phone. Take a selfie, what they call a "bathroom selfie," and look in the mirror. Now take a look at the picture. Do you see how your eyes are not really looking straight forward? You're really looking slightly off-camera. Now this time, try it again, and look into the mirror but focus on where the phone's camera lens is located. Focus exactly there in the mirror. Snap the shot. You will see that this time, it looks like you were taking the picture directly into the mirror.

It matters where you focus your eyes and your attention.

It matters in a selfie, it matters to the audience, and it matters to you. Just like taking a selfie, if you focus appropriately during a presentation, you will make a direct connection with your audience. If you don't, you will look and feel off-center and off-target.

Are you ready for one of the most important sentences in this entire book? Here it is. *To make the best connection with your audience, you must know where to focus.* Whether or not you are speaking, being silent, taking questions, or listening, you need to build your perception and connection skills until you can be present and properly focused in your communication.

This means you have to choose your focal points carefully. Eye contact alone will no longer do; you have to learn to see inside their spirits, and more importantly, let them see inside yours. The magic happens when we cultivate curiosity and learn to know each other. Does this all sound daunting and even a little weird? I can see how it might. But I will say one thing: Get over it. As a society, as a world, we are starving for connection, and many of us have forgotten how to connect in an authentic and substantive way. We must re-learn these skills of perception and connection. The best communicators excel at them.

And it isn't just about learning how to read people. We can all learn how to read people – we can do cold readings, or we can pick up a copy of Dale Carnegie's *How to Win Friends and Influence People*. That's relatively easy. The hard part is to allow people to know us. We must allow ourselves to be vulnerable to others. We must open ourselves and be willing to connect, show our true selves, warts and all.

I can't stress this enough: The more authentic and intimate your connection with your audience, the more you will be able to speak directly from your heart to their hearts. This is crucial. They have to know you are there with them and for them. If they do, they will trust you to the ends of the Earth, because they'll realize you have only their best interest at heart. And if they don't, there will always be a separation between you. It might be fine and gauzy, or it might be an almost-tangible barrier. If you are not open and willing to be vulnerable with your audience, you'll damage your ability to connect with them.

After all, that's what it's all about. You are there to share a piece of your heart and soul. You are the person presenting, connecting, and communicating. If you are not real, if you are not intimate and authentic, you will turn them off. And then you might as well not have shown up.

It won't be easy. Once we are adults, we might feel like we know pretty much everything we need to know. So, in order for us to feel safe admitting ignorance of any sort, we must open and unpack that tender part of ourselves. We need to be willing to be fragile, and fragility is hard to come by with coworkers or strangers in an audience. And sometimes it's most difficult to share with those you love best. If you feel like you must always be the dependable and stalwart one, then fragility becomes a vulnerability – which brings me back to my point: It's not just eye contact. It's heart-to-heart contact, and we need to know how to do it. We need to know how to do it when we walk into a room prepared to meet new people one-on-one or to give a speech to thousands. We must be willing to be vulnerable first, in order for our listeners to be willing to be vulnerable with us.

Figure out for yourself what you need to be open and vulnerable with your audience. Now, I don't mean that you should go in there and start weeping. You can be open and vulnerable without being a crying mess. (Though if this is not an arena where you can be vulnerable in that way, I advise you to keep that part under wraps.) But somewhere in each of us, there lives a part that is seeking, wondering, and learning. It wants to connect with others so that we can blossom in a shared spirit of growth and progress.

Before I walk on stage or in front of a class or seminar group, I spend time in meditation, and I say a prayer. It goes something like this: "May I speak from my heart. May I listen with my spirit. May we connect and be as one, so I can help them learn and strive and thrive. May this be for the good of all and may it harm none. So I have spoken, so it shall be done. May this or something better come to pass."

I make a promise to myself, to my audience, and to the universe at large that I will endeavor to be present with them and to help them to the best of my ability. I am reminded right now of that golden nugget: Under-promise and over-deliver. If you connect with your audience on these deepest, intimate, and vulnerable levels, together you will make miracles.

Mission: Talk to Strangers

I'm going to encourage you to do something that might feel strange. For the next three days, look strangers in the eye (paying attention to cultural norms and always using good safety precautions. Please take care of yourself and don't initiate any sort of contact or connection if it feels at all unsafe.). And if you see a spark in them, pay them a compliment. It doesn't have to be physical. Just let them know that you recognize that they have a spark. You might say they seem very confident. You might tell them they're handsome or beautiful. You don't have to say anything else, but if it feels safe, make that connection.

Allow yourself the vulnerability of connecting to the delicate inner heart of others. And I can guarantee you, if you tell someone that you recognize their spark, they will recognize yours. Build that awareness and skill. And when you are in front of a room of hundreds, you will extend that skill outward until it touches every person in that space.

Then, we know we are present and connected. Then we know that a true exchange of information, energy, sizzle, and light can occur. That's what it takes. It takes us being vulnerable to get to a place where people will feel confident enough in us to share, connect, and learn.

Mission: Smile at Strangers

This is another exercise for you if the first one feels too daunting for now. It's about focal points. Until you are ready to be vulnerable enough to see inside the other person's heart and open your heart for them to see inside yours, try quick eye contact with a slight smile. See what that feels like. When you're walking by strangers on the street, make eye contact and smile. That's all. Unless you feel ready and enthusiastic and extroverted, don't go grinning right now. You might not be ready for that. But a small smile to indicate that something in you recognizes something in them will open a world of connection.

I'll say it again. Be open. Be real. Be who you are. Be vulnerable and reach out from that tender place. You do that, and you will make strong, healthy connections for life. Will you connect with every person in the room? Likely not. But you'll touch more than a few and you will all be enriched by the experience.

11 CONNECTION AND CURIOSITY

We have gotten away from the knowledge, the certainty, that we are all connected. I'm not sure when we left it behind. It seems like nowadays it takes special effort to recognize that another person, or other people, are just like us. Maybe it's that we have a huge population on this planet. Maybe it's that we're afraid that if we are open and vulnerable that we are leaving ourselves bare to be hurt or worse. But I can't help feeling that in order to find that common ground that lets us meet each other in that fragile and crucial place, we must acknowledge that we are all connected.

Smarter people than I have said the same thing. Most of our DNA is shared among the tiniest bacteria. We share 99 and some odd percent of our DNA with chimpanzees. We share even more than that with every single human on the planet. When we look into each other's eyes and see ourselves reflected there, I can't help thinking we must accept that we are all the same. And when we do that, we will realize that every one of us has similar needs. Each one of us needs love, shelter, protection, security, adventure – and, I believe, the opportunity to create and express ourselves.

If we're all seeking similar goals, how hard then is it to

think about that when we stand before each other and speak our truth? Can we reach that same soft, tender core in the people listening to us? If we can meet there, we can show each other true understanding. And this isn't so much about what you say to them when you communicate – it's more about listening to what they need to say to you.

Go with me on this. Most of the time, when we speak to others, we're the ones doing the talking. But here's an idea: Instead, what if we started every speech, every spoken word, by being authentically curious about the people listening to us? What if we started everything with curiosity? What if we asked them questions? And what if that informed not only how we spoke but also what we spoke about?

How's that for a radical notion? It's an important one. We talked earlier about the importance of researching your audience – I never start any speech or presentation without knowing something about the people to whom I'm speaking, but I also start every presentation with the following question: "What I'd like to do before we begin, is to ask you all to tell me a little something about yourselves." Now, what I ask differs depending on whether I'm teaching a singing workshop, a communication or negotiation seminar, or a writing workshop. But it's always designed to help me learn about my audience. Who are these people who have taken the time to give me their attention? Could they have instead gone sightseeing? Might they have hightailed it to a museum, the zoo, or a bar? Absolutely, they could have. Instead, they're here and ready to be part of our journey.

So, I ask. "Who are you? What do you do for fun? What is your level of experience about subject matter X?" And then I ask the doozy: "What do you hope to get out of this talk?"

If I'm speaking in front of 500 people, I can't ask them all individually unless we're doing a three-day event – and even then, it would be problematic – so I ask them beforehand. I send them a pre-talk survey. If I am speaking to people who all share a characteristic, I do some research. If they belong to the same group or organization, I find information on their mission, ideals, and status. It's always a good idea find out who these people are and what they love to do. If I know what they love, I can find the threads that will tie my life to their lives. And as soon as I have that common ground, I can forge that connection.

If you do this research before your next communication opportunity, please remember why you are doing it. You are looking to find the common threads you have with your audience so you can better engage them. Did you go to the same college? Do you like the same sports team? Do you share a love of cupcakes? Are you both Key West aficionados? What are the things that give you a touchstone? What are your commonalities? Remember, if we are all connected, all you have to do is figure out what those connections are.

As I said above, we all have certain commonalities. Chances are, the people to whom you will be speaking put on clothes this morning. Likely, they will eat something today. They probably own a cell phone. They might be in a relationship. We can strike a chord of similarity in many ways – but we're not interested in the surface similarities. They're a starting point, but we want authentic similarity. And that can be frightening, because those similarities come from a connection that goes deeper. It comes from the fact that we all likely want love and joy in our lives. We all probably had childhood dreams. We wanted to be something when we grew up. We all have a certain amount of pain that we carry around. Some of it is from old hurts, regrets, or from broken dreams. Some of it is the thing we never said or did.

We all also show tremendous courage every day that we get up and do, work, live, and strive.

That commonality – that thread – is gold. And I don't mean just that it's valuable. It's also fragile. We must respect that we all have shared pain. Some of us live in much more pain than others. Some of us maintain a daily facade that hides our true feelings. But if we remove the facade, if we even allude to removing it, it can make for fireworks.

So, I'm not telling you to go ahead and rip the bandage off of other people's wounds. I am telling you to find within yourself a well of understanding for whatever pain other people around you might be going through. There's not a single one of us who doesn't have some pain. And that's OK. If we all have this as a commonality, then we all can meet each other in that place and guide each other from it to a place that is better, healthier, and more healed. Remember, the worst we have to deal with is the worst we have to deal with. No one has the market cornered on pain or tough times. If we can understand that, we can all emerge victorious.

Empathy

Right now, we're talking about having empathy for your audience. Empathy is the acknowledgement of someone else's experience. Notice, I'm not saying that we need to feel or express sorrow in these situations. That is actually more a sympathetic response than an empathetic one. When we have empathy, we are able to see and understand what someone else is going through. And we can also deepen our level of empathy and incorporate it into every single interaction we have with anyone. Remember, this is a shared adventure. We all come into this arena from different doors and with different experiences, but we're all in it together. Each one of us has a different role, but still, we're all in it together.

12 KNOW YOUR ROLE

What do I mean by "Know your role?" Let me give you an example. When I was a child, my family spent time with a small community of friends. When we went to someone else's house for a dinner party, upon walking in with whatever guesting gift we were bringing, my mother found the hostess and offered to help. She became the person who helped lay out the dishes on the table, or she offered drinks. She became a seamless and critical component of the gathering. And then she was busy for the rest of the evening.

After one such party, when my mom had spent the bulk of the evening putting out dishes of food and bussing the tables, I wanted to know why she spent so many parties working.

"Aren't you a guest like everyone else?" I asked her. "Yes," she responded. "But I'm shy with new people. And if I have a job to do, I have something to talk with them about."

Aha! What an educational moment. My mom was shy. Small talk didn't come easily to her, and getting to know people made her anxious. However, if she had a job to do, things went more smoothly. She had an easier time because she knew her role. She could inhabit the role of the person who bussed the tables or put out the food, and that increased her ease and facilitated her interactions with new people. So it's not just altruism that moves people to offer help – sometimes, it's a subconscious need to know their role.

Try it the next time you're feeling anxious in a public situation. Find the person in charge and ask, "What can I do to help?"

Most likely they'll smile, breathe a sigh of relief, and give you a job. Once you have that job, you can approach the rest of the time you're there from the perspective of someone who has that job. All your interactions can be based on that, and in the meantime, you can be getting to know people. You can connect with them through the lens of your role. Chances are that role will not be your profession, but once people know your role and know you're there to help out, you can start introducing other subjects. You will already have a connection, so the rest of the conversation will have an easier flow. As an added bonus, you will bring value to your host or hostess, and that's always a great thing.

Here's a fun example from my own life. Periodically, I get to go back to my theatre roots and take jobs playing characters for various talent agencies in the Washington D.C. area. Once, I was hired to play a maid for a 1960s-garden-party-themed wedding reception. (Yes, I wore a maid's outfit. See it here – https://IzoldaT.com/speak-book/ under Chapter 12 heading.)

There were dozens of characters, and we were all doing something different, but there were two other women, both of whom were maids for the same "manor." We were supposed to have some interaction with guests and we were supposed to be "cleaning" and straightening the lounge while the guests milled about. I realized quickly that there was only so much "cleaning" I could do in the space. So, I was going to have to come up with a different set of "duties."

I didn't wait for someone to assign me a particular role. I took one. This was a fancy affair, with gold filigree name cards set up on a grand table festooned with a centerpiece that was over six feet tall. I decided to take on the role of the person who made sure that every single card was perfectly aligned in rows and alphabetized. When someone came to take one of the filigreed cards, I realigned each one, dusted the area, and fussed until each card was back exactly as it should be. After a few minutes, the guests realized that I was the go-to person to find their cards. I had some incredibly fun interactions with people as I deftly navigated the throng of guests, found their cards, and presented them with a flourish. And then I would align the cards once again, alphabetizing them and placing them exactly two inches apart.

Many a guest told me I was hilarious as I wound around the room, got the names of guests, made sure I pronounced the names correctly, in a proper and prim accent, and then went about my "busy-ness" of setting the table back to rights. I studied the table with a critical eye from all the angles and made sure all the cards were perfectly neat while I waited for the next guests to ask for theirs. The guests had fun interacting with me, and we all had a grand time connecting and playing with one another.

As an actor, it was a sensible character choice. I was able to don the cloak of the prim and proper – but extremely competent – maid. And, as part of that character, I interacted with guests, made them laugh, and still did "my job."

It also gave me a way, as a communicator and speaker, to connect with guests and communicate with them in a fun and lighthearted way. All the while, we deepened our connection as people through entertainment and laughter. I didn't have a role, to begin with. My first 15 to 20 minutes were spent dusting, and I realized while that was an OK choice as an actor, it was not ideal. Once I had a role, my interactions deepened, became more entertaining, and created a connection that allowed everyone to have a more fulfilling time.

Think about it: Isn't that our role when we go to meet and speak with new people? Aren't we supposed to put them at ease, connect with them, and communicate on those deeper levels? If we know our roles, or if we take them on until we are comfortable in our own skins, we can build those connections. And let me be honest – if you have that connection, everything else will blossom from there.

Training

By the way, I don't think you have to be a trained actor in order to wear a role. You just need to think about it. You have to flesh it out for yourself. The roles I'm talking about here are not Hamlet or Hedda Gabler. They are the ones you can find within yourself, so you can be real while still being the person who knows how to do what you need to do.

If what we're talking about is meeting new people, you need to take on the role of someone who is comfortable doing that. At a gathering of friends, you might be the person who offers to pick up drinks or bus the table. At a corporate event, you might be the person who knows how to direct everyone to the restroom. Or you might know the tastiest tidbit in the array of hors-d'oeuvres. You will have to choose what works for you.

Perhaps, you will be the person who knows the program for the evening inside and out. You will be able to discuss it, and you will be able to direct others to what they need to know. Pick something. You can look at the event through the lens of that role. It all happens when you assess the situation and marry it to your skills. Figure out what will be the biggest help to everyone there, and you'll enrich everyone's experience as a result. Remember, people love people who solve their problems. If you are scared to interact, become a problem-solver, and you will be among the most popular people in the place.

Mission: Choose Your Role

The next time you attend a party, whether or not you feel shy or anxious, identify a role for yourself. Perhaps, you will be the drink order taker or the mixologist. You might be the food freshener, the table busser, or the coat-taker. This last one works great because you will see people when they arrive and when they leave. This will give you a chance to chat about small things during the first interaction but deeper things during the second one.

Find a role that works for your personality and be that role for the duration of the event. Pay attention to your interactions. Notice their quality and characteristics. Are they deeper than usual? Are they less in-depth? Study them. Become a behavioral scientist and evaluate how you feel and how you behave. Most of all, assess your comfort level during any interactions with strangers. Do things feel easier if you have a role? I'll bet they feel a ton easier. That ease can make all the difference in a meeting, interview, or a presentation for your business or next promotion. You must have the confidence to start – and sometimes, you need a little acting flair to help you along.

Acting 101

If you weren't lucky enough to take a good acting or drama class in school, you might consider signing up for one now. (I'm going to offer an online acting course at some point.) Actors like Helen Mirren also have online courses to help you learn: https://www.masterclass.com/classes/helen-mirren-teaches-acting.

However, at the least, you can start thinking of yourself as an actor who just happens to be playing the role of yourself. As you get to know yourself better, you'll flesh out the role, and you will connect more deeply with every audience.

13 DIALOGUE

I was teaching a writing workshop one time, and I mentioned dialogue. I said that when you write dialogue in books, it's not like a regular conversation. It's more like conversation-plus. When we write dialogue for books, we don't put in "ums" or fits and starts. Most of the time, people are clever – or if they aren't clever, there's a specific reason for them not to be. The dialogue in a book streaks by. It's rapid-fire. It's smart. It can be pithy. (Look at Terry Pratchett's books.) Seldom is it boring, mundane, or insipid – unless the character is supposed to be boring in which case, that's OK.

Unfortunately, in our regular lives, we often talk about the shopping list or whose turn it is to clean the bathroom. In books, movies, and television, not so much – usually people are saying something passionate, inspiring, funny, or angry. Sometimes it's something evil, but even then it's passionate. So, in literature, movies, books, and TV, it's all conversation-plus.

The same thing must hold true for presentations, meetings, interviews, and any other communication that isn't sitting around with friends and shooting the breeze. We must make that communication more exciting, more authentic, and more captivating than the average shopping list.

What does that mean for you as you navigate the landscape of being a good communicator? It means you have to pay attention, be authentic, and be ready to listen, learn, and speak in any situation. I don't mean you have to know it all. I mean you have to know who you are, so that you can be that person with your audience in an instant.

When you walk into any sort of communication situation, you need to have your conversation-plus antenna up and ready to go. Ideally, you will be as much a listener as you will be a talker. Your conversation will need to be thoughtful and purposeful. You will need to speak with focus and towards a point. Why? Because, again, this isn't your average everyday conversation. You are either trying to shine, trying to convince your listeners of something, or trying to reach them so that your connection deepens and becomes more intimate.

You can learn and practice a number of acting exercises that will help you establish the connection quickly.

Mission: Word for Word

Try this with a friend and see how long you can go. This simple exercise/activity helps you see how your minds work and how in sync you can get as you increase your speed. The first person says a word, any word. Through a stream of consciousness, the other person responds with a word that is somehow related. The first person adds another word. You exchange Word for Word to make two-word phrases and see how far you get. Please note: This is as much a listening exercise as it is a speaking one. It will help you build both a receiving and sending skill. You will laugh, a lot. The game ends when you somehow bring it back around to the original word. Here's an example.

Person one: Star
Person two: Star Wars
Person one: wars suck
Person two: suck straws
Person one straws drawn
Person two: drawn stars

As you open your mind to the stream of consciousness between you and play with how you generate ideas, you will deepen your connection and build your listening and speaking skills.

You can also do it with three words where you repeat the first one and then add two more. Here is an example.

Person one: mermaids
Person two: mermaids swim
Person one: mermaids swim nightly
Person two: swim nightly careful
Person one: nightly careful to
Person two: careful to walk
Person one: to walk on
Person two: walk on Shores
Person one: on Shores far
Person two: Shores far away
Person one: far away where
Person two: away where mermaids
Person one: where mermaids swim.

Because you listened to each other, you might come up with a story that works beautifully, a poignant moment when your speak-and-listen created a bit of magic.

"Mermaids swim nightly careful to walk on shores far away where mermaids swim."

Mission: Emotional Word for Word

Here is another give-and-take, send/receive/speak/listen activity that builds on what you just did. Find a trusted friend and try these until you feel confident that you're receiving the other person's true intent. Then, you can send your true intent. You're telling a story as before, but this time, decide beforehand whether your random beginning, middle, and end will be funny, tragic, thrilling, exciting, or romantic. Then use your words to create the theme and meaning as you give and take rapid-fire. This makes it more of a theatre game, but it will change how you view the conversation. You can't go too slowly as that will kill the pace of the give-and-take. And you can't go too quickly, or your words won't fulfill the criteria.

Have you noticed how much of this book calls on you to be proactive in your own growth? I wish that I could wave a magic wand and help you accept and love yourself, to feel truly deserving of success and joy and happiness. But, like most of us, you probably have some work to do in that arena. That's OK. We all have things we can improve in the way we approach our inner landscape.

This will mean doing the exercises, reaching into the well of your own spirit, finding what lives there and making friends with it. You will connect with others, yes, but you'll also do some housekeeping of your own.

14 LISTEN AND LEARN

When you are engaged in public speaking, your listening and perception skills are more important than your speaking skills. Don't get me wrong – speaking skills are crucial. What you say, how you say it, and the way you frame both – physically, emotionally and psychologically – makes a huge difference. However, how you listen is crucial to knowing your role. If someone needs a shoulder to lean on, you can't come in like a freight train. You must sense what they need, and then give it to them in the way they need it.

Examine your perception skills. It doesn't have to be in a public speaking situation, or an interview or any other kind of speaking event. Rather, test your abilities on the people closest to you. Spend time listening and see what you pick up below the surface. That's where true communication happens.

A few years ago, I was at a festival. I decided that I would spend almost no time talking about myself. Instead, I would focus all of my attention on the people I met. I would plumb the depths and see what treasures I could find. Every time I met a new person, I spent every moment being curious, asking questions, and listening. I seldom talked. The only talking I did for five days was to encourage other people to talk about themselves. And you know what? Dozens of people told me that I was a brilliant conversationalist. How funny, since I said almost nothing. For them, having a skilled listener made them feel that they were speaking to someone adept in the communication arts.

I'll be honest. While I love technology and I respect everything that it does for us, I believe that it has also created a certain amount of isolation. We spend a lot of time putting out or consuming content on social media. We spend an incredible amount of time presenting a facade of who we might want to be, rather than who we actually are in the moment. And we do it with a keyboard or a phone. Seldom do we see each other face-to-face, even in our most intimate interactions.

As a result, we are not honing our skills. In fact, our abilities around awareness and perception are decreasing. On top of that, what we see on social media might not be authentic – it might just be an image of the life the poster wants us to believe they have. Because it comes through via a screen, we are once removed from presence and intimacy. We have to guess what someone is thinking or feeling behind the facade of their latest status update. So when we try to perceive, evaluate, and react to stimuli, we don't have a lot to go on.

That makes me nervous. It makes room for less kindness in the world. If we can be removed from the frailty and the vulnerability of others, we can ignore their needs and even their pain. But if we want to be authentic communicators, we cannot afford to ignore anyone's vulnerability – especially our own.

Mission: Eye to Eye

Here is another exercise. You can try this with a trusted friend, or you can do it by yourself with a mirror. It's simple, but tricky. Sit with your friend and look into each other's eyes. Do nothing else. Sit, breathe, and gaze into each other's eyes. Assess how you feel. See what comes up for you as you engage with one another. I will bet that after just a few minutes, one of you will begin to giggle. Your eyes will water. You will have an itch on your nose, or you will laugh because you're looking at someone else's face for no good reason.

Once you get past the laughter phase, you might notice that something more tender bubbles up. You might notice something quieter, softer, and more fragile extends between you and your partner. Explore it for a moment. See how you feel to sit together and share this tender moment. Shortly after that, you might giggle again, but I guarantee you will know each other a little better. And you will love each other a little more.

If you decide to do this exercise on your own, find a quiet time at home. Stand in front of the bathroom mirror or if you have another sit in front of it and stare into your own eyes. Try to work through the "I feel stupid" thoughts that will spring up. Give yourself permission to admire yourself. In fact, pay yourself a compliment. For many of us, that's easy to do on the surface. It's much harder to go deep, locate that fragile place, and connect with it.

Find something about your face that appeals to you and either think it or say it out loud. It can be something as simple as "I like your hair today," or "You have a nice smile." Don't be afraid to pay yourself a real gem. You deserve it. You are entitled to love and admiration and appreciation. Sometimes, in the hustle and bustle of our daily lives, we forget that we are worthwhile, deserving, and lovable beings. And here's one of the biggest secrets of the universe: The more we feel like we are worthwhile, deserving, and lovable, the more we will extend those feelings to others when we communicate with them.

Those feelings will bring us peace, joy, and every good little thing.

I could devote an entire book to the paying of a compliment and how it affects both the surface and the innermost being of the person who receives it. I could also talk about how much it brings to the person who gives it. When you find the strength and the vulnerability within yourself to take a chance and pay a compliment, to extend yourself to offer up kind or admiring words unsolicited, you are doing a very brave and courageous thing. I know. I do it every day.

The Compliment Project

Every day that I am out and about I pay a random stranger a compliment. I try to remain observant of the people around me, because it's a good idea to know who is where, and a few years ago, I took it a step further. When something strikes me about a person, I will comment on it and compliment them with no ulterior motive other than to acknowledge that I think something about them is wonderful. They might be in line at the coffee shop. We might both be at the post office. It doesn't matter where we are. If I notice that someone has a great smile or lovely eyes or is wearing a cool outfit, I point it out and let them know I think they are terrific. And here's the thing. If you extend yourself to someone, they might accept it with honesty and maybe even gratitude, or they might rebuff and ridicule you. If you maintain your composure and don't give up or quit, you will build and increase your sense of self. Thus, the Compliment Project serves multiple purposes. It brightens other people's days, and it helps me stretch and grow.

These compliments I've paid over the years have never been rebuffed. I have never had anyone tell me I was crazy, or tell me to stop coming on to them, or any other of the possible responses you might receive when paying a stranger a compliment out of the blue. It's possible that something like that will happen. In fact, I'm sure it will happen. So, I recognize that someone will react badly someday. And I need to know how to deal with that. However, the compliments portion of our show has always resulted in eyes opening a little wider and a big smile and usually some sort of a surprised "Thank you!"

Why are they surprised? I think it's because we are no longer used to hearing compliments. We're more used to hearing insults, criticism or critique, so a compliment knocks us for a loop. Ideally, I would like to bring that practice back as a daily occurrence. I want it to be so commonplace that we no longer even think about responding with scorn or rejection. Rather, we build everyone up until we all feel deserving of the compliments. Then, when someone pays us one, instead of being shocked, amazed, or surprised, we are able to take it in and say a sincere "thank you." I think we deserve it. Don't you?

And yes, I will add that this must be done with pure intent. We ought not to use it as a come-on. If you have that energy inside you as you go to pay the compliment, don't do it. Move on. This compliment should be from the heart, from your spirit to theirs. It's not a stop on the flirting train. In fact, right after you pay the compliment to someone, move along. **This isn't about flirting or hooking up with anyone. This is about connecting with someone on a deeper level.** You let them know you appreciate them – and then you walk right past them, so you can both live your lives enriched by the experience and free of any other expectations.

It ought to start small, though. I think we could start it with compliments to ourselves. That "look in the mirror and tell yourself you're fabulous" exercise? It's harder than it seems. Sure, it's easy to do in a perfunctory way. It's easier to stand there and say the words "you're beautiful" or "you're gorgeous" or "you're intelligent" or "you are lovable." But to say it to yourself and mean it? That's a different story. It can take some of us weeks, months, or years to get to where we can pay ourselves a compliment and accept it – and here's another secret no one tells you: It is much, much easier to sincerely compliment someone else, anyone else, then it is to compliment ourselves. Now, we don't know how the person we compliment actually reacts. They might say "pish" and brush the words aside. Or it might make them pause long enough for a bit of that intention to seep in.

I would say the second hardest thing in that interaction is to take the compliment in. The easiest? To say it. We do have to get over some blocks on that. We do have to figure out how to say those words without any fear, expectation, judgment, or even jealousy. We have to get to a place where we can remark on our admiration for someone else's qualities without feeling a pinch of either guilt or sorrow that either we don't feel that way, or that we weren't on the receiving end. Because the truth is, receiving a compliment feels good, even if it feels odd. If someone takes the time to do that for us authentically and without an ulterior motive, that might be a beautiful thing. What I'm describing here is a way for all of us to develop a connection through positive means. We must release any expectation of something more coming from the interaction. It is a means of connecting us on a platonic yet universal level. I use it as a sort of meditative practice, because it allows me to maintain an awareness of the people around me and to remain in an attitude of thoughtful presence and joy when I pay compliments.

We also have to release the fear of being rebuffed, because there's a flip side to this coin, and I'm going tell you about it. I'm one of those people who believes in being helpful. Sometimes, when you're trying to be helpful and trying to communicate and to offer whatever aid you can, you'll be rebuffed and ridiculed. You have to be prepared to handle those situations, both as they are happening and in your soul afterward.

Here's my story about that: A few years ago, I was at Ruby Tuesday's, standing in line at the salad bar. A father and son were in line directly in front of me. For those of you who might not know, Ruby Tuesday's has big television screens that show various sports events or news channels. The father and son were complaining as we went through the line. They were bummed that their game, the one they wanted to watch, was not the one being televised on the screen where they were sitting.

"Excuse me," I said. "I couldn't help but overhear. I'm sure that if you ask your waiter, they would be happy to change the channel for you to one that has your game on it." I offered the advice because I knew that they would be willing to change channels – I'd asked them before myself.

"What the f*ck are you doing listening to our conversation?" the father snarled. "Mind your own goddamn business."

"I was trying to help," I said.

"I don't need any of your damn help," he said. Do you want to know what saddened me the most? He did this in front of his teenaged son.

No, wait. I just lied to you. Here's the thing that upset me the most: It was the son's response.

He looked at his father with adoration in his eyes and he said, "I love you, Dad."

As a person, I weep for the son. As a communicator, I'm shocked at the lessons that father was teaching his child.

Honest communication and compassion will be challenging for him as he grows into a man. He will have trouble gaining other people's trust. Sure, this blustery and quick-to-anger style might win him some short-term gains. But I'll bet dollars to doughnuts that he'll have a tough time finding true happiness and success in the long-run. Some people might believe in him to begin with, but they will move along once they learn his values.

The entrepreneur Malcolm Forbes once said, "You can easily judge the character of a man by how he treats those who can do nothing for him." It appears to me that this child will face some harsh realities if he treats people the way his father is teaching him to.

Honestly, that moment saddened me, and it stunted my desire to interact with strangers; for a few weeks, I hesitated to help people when I saw their need. I usually get involved when it looks like someone needs help, because I think we can all use a helping hand. But for those few weeks, I stopped. I stopped because a part of me feared a repeat of what had happened. But then I realized that I had been helping strangers for years, and this was the only time it had caused me pain. Every other time the people I tried to aid met me without anger. Sometimes, they accepted my help. Sometimes, they didn't. But no one had ever been so harsh and rude. The problem wasn't with me or my desire to help others. The problem lay with that man and his son. I was sorry I couldn't help them, but I also couldn't hold onto the pain the interaction had caused.

I decided that the best way for me to feel better about that entire situation was to turn right around and try to help someone else. I adhere to the notion that if I fall off a bike, I have to get right back on and start pedaling. And here's how I did just that.

A few weeks later, my husband and I had stopped at a small store along MacArthur Boulevard in Washington, D.C. (an area where there are few stores). A man and his son walked in right after us. The man staggered to the cashier and asked if they had any Advil. He had a terrible headache and was clearly suffering.

"No, we don't carry anything like that," the cashier responded.

I reached into my purse and pulled out a small container of the tablets.

"Here you go, sir," I extended the pillbox toward him.

"What? No, I can't take your Advil," he said.

"Please," I said. "Take it. I know what it's like to be in that kind of pain."

"Yeah, she does this kind of thing," my husband said to him. "So, you should just take them."

"Thank you!" The man accepted the tablets and downed them.

"No problem," I answered. And you know what? He wasn't the only one who felt better.

Trustworthy Selflessness

At its core, communication requires a sort of trustworthy selflessness. We must put our own needs and desire to express ourselves second to the needs of those with whom we are communicating. We must listen and perceive. We must also empathize. We must be able to put ourselves in the shoes of the people who are our audience. Their number doesn't matter. If we are going to communicate with them on that most important of levels, we will need to connect, or it won't work. Let me rephrase that – it might work in the short-term, but in the long-term, the fakers will lose. So, be true to yourself and to your audience. Use your perceptive skills to connect and then be authentic in your dealings with them.

15 "LET ME HEAR YOUR BODY TALK"

Am I dating myself too much with this chapter title? I'm ok with that, though. Who are we if we can't laugh at ourselves?

Let's talk about body language. Sheryl Sandberg wrote a great book called *Lean In*, and by "lean in," she means that to show our level of engagement and interest in our interactions, we must lean forward. Lean towards the goal. Lean towards the challenge. Lean towards the interaction. If you are excited, if you are engaged, you will do that. If you act more reserved, you might sit with legs crossed or arms crossed. If you are relaxed or lethargic, you might lean back in your seat and sprawl. Word to the wise: If you are the one in the hot seat, don't sprawl.

No, wait. If you are interviewing for a position at a surf shop, you might just want to do that. If on the other hand, you're walking into a meeting to propose a radical change in the way your company does business, you probably will stand and present using strong, confident body language.

Feel free to move around when you speak in public. In some cultures, using your hands to gesticulate is considered taboo, so do your research. But for the most part, using your body to emphasize your points is powerful. It also gives your voice a bigger instrument. Do you remember what I said about how our bodies are our resonance chambers? When you use your body and you move, you change the chamber through which your voice emanates. It's like having a different and more dynamic instrument. Movement of any sort will help your voice come through.

Mission: Vocalize an Ah

If you're comfortable standing, stand with your feet hip-width apart, your spine straight and your hands at your sides. (Note: if you are not comfortable standing, you can do this while sitting. Sit with your feet flat on the floor and hip-width apart and your spine straight.) Take one of the deep breaths we've talked about before and make an Ah sound. I recommend you try it on your own first so that you can feel and hear the difference before you watch the video and see the difference. (Watch the video at https://IzoldaT.com/speak-book under the Chapter 15 heading.) As you stand and make the sound, keep your hands at your sides. Do it a couple of times, and you will get an awareness of what you sound like.

After you've gotten used to that, try this. Still standing with your hands at your sides, start the Ah sound. While you are voicing it, let your arms rise up to shoulder height. Notice what happens to your Ah sound. Don't change the Ah on purpose. Just notice what happens to it. Try it a few times. After you've run through that a few times and have gotten used to it, start at the beginning and try the following: Sound the Ah, and as you're voicing it allow your arms to lift up until they are over your head, making a V for victory sign. Again, notice the quality of the sound. Did it change? Can you describe it?

I'm betting you noticed how much louder and fuller your voice got as you raised your arms. In terms of physics, you created a bigger sound chamber. In terms of energy, you gave your voice more room to play. Both worked together to give you a rich, full sound. A lot of what happens when we try to speak is that nervousness constricts our entire body – and it doesn't just constrict the physical body, it constricts the energetic body as well.

The Energetic Body

You know how you instantly know that someone is behind you even though they've made no noise? Let's say you're busy reading a book or writing a book or sitting and meditating. It doesn't matter. You're quiet and still. Someone comes up behind you. You don't hear or see them, and yet you know they are there. That's the energetic body at work. Our senses are not just sight, smell, touch, etc. We also have something called the kinesthetic sense – and the kinesthetic sense is all about motion.

In physics, energy that is in motion is kinetic, so the kinesthetic sense is our awareness of the energetic motion of things around us. How do we sense those things? What do we use to sense them? It's not about what we can hear, though that might play a role. It's not about what we can see either. You would need to have someone announce they are there – or eyes in the back of your head – to know that they'd come near without sensing them any other way. However, your energetic body can do it.

The energetic body is a kind of a field around you that extends however far you want it to extend. At rest, without specific direction from you, it's probably a couple of feet. But it doesn't have to be that small. One of the things that we are never taught anymore – because we have been taught to rely on our tangible senses – is how to work with and utilize the energetic body both for sending and receiving information.

The energetic body can sense the flow of heat and other energy around us. It can sense danger and joy. It can sense a change in the energy of the space around us. Have you ever walked into a room in which everyone was still, silent, or busy, but you've known something was wrong? That's your energetic body talking to you. Everybody sends energy out;

your energy picks it up and vice versa. We might not understand the message right away, but we can start to build that awareness.

I could write an entire book about building the skill of energetic body awareness, but let me start by saying you can hone your skills with a couple of simple exercises, which I often teach people in my workshops.

Here's something that happened during one of my "Speak From Within" workshops, covering a lot of the principles you're learning in this book.

"So one of the things that we can do is talk about the energetic body," I told the class. "Does anybody know what I mean when I say the energetic body?"

One of the students spoke up. "I'm assuming you're referring to body language, how the person moves, for instance, when you cross your arms like this, you're trying to keep people away?"

"Yes, keep people away. Yeah, things like that." I replied. "Unless you're from a part of the world where this is an engaging thing. And there are parts of the world where this is engaging and we need to know something about whom we're dealing with, but we also need to know the messages they're giving us in the moment. And I'm going to do a little exercise with you. Who would like to be my lucky volunteer? Come on up, Stacy," I encouraged the student who had raised her hand. "Stand way over there," I pointed her towards one end of the room.

"This is a very simple test. Just stand and face me. And you're going to see us relate, and you're going to see what happens when I get in the space of her energetic body," I said to the class. "You ready?" I moved to the other side of the room. Watching Stacy, I walked towards her.

"Okay. Did you see it? What happened to her face?" I asked the rest of the class.

"She smiled."

"She smiled," I agreed. "Okay. Watch again. Ready?"

"I'm trying not to smile," Stacy said. The rest of the class giggled.

"You just be you," I instructed. "And they're going to watch you like hawks. Are you ready?"

"Okay," she nodded.

I walked towards her once more.

"She smiled even more," one of the students stated.

"She smiled even more. Right?" I turned to Stacy. "And you're going, 'I don't want to smile. I'm not gonna smile.' And you can't help it. I am way in her personal space right now, aren't I?" I asked the class. "I'm in the bubble of her energetic body. This is where her personal space started, and we can tell that by the first time she smiled, right? Right here," I pointed to a spot about six feet in front of Stacy.

"Here's the thing," I continued. "The more I can pay attention to those nonverbal cues, the more I know where she is. And there are certain parts of the world where you can get a lot closer, and you're not in people's personal space. And there are certain parts of the world where you need to be a lot further. You have to know what the right distance is so that you can be appropriate to the people you're talking to. Does that make sense?"

Again, I walked to the other side of the room.

"Now, here's what I'm going to do," I announced. "We have access to our energetic body, and we can actually use it how we want to use it. We can invite people in closer, or we can keep them back, and we can actually do that with our own intention. So I'm going to ask you to do one more thing for me," I addressed Stacy. "Somewhere between us, I want you to set up where you think you want me to stop. Okay? And I'm going to walk, and we're going to see if I can tell where she wants me to stop. It can be the same place, but it doesn't have to be. Okay? You ready?"

"Okay."

"Are you all ready? Oh and it's not about smiling, you'll see. You will see her actually back up a little. You'll see it happen. Did you watch it happen last time?"

"Yes," they chorused.

"Her body kind of went backward, and it's unconscious. It's not something we know we're doing. You ready?"

She nodded and I walked towards her once more. I stopped cold about seven feet away.

"Yeah, right there. Right about there. And I'm in the middle. I could take that next step, I think I'd be right in the spot, where Stacy would be thinking, 'No, don't come closer.' And we can build our awareness so that we know, even if I'm here, and we're talking," I took one step closer. "Did you watch what she just did?" I asked, and the class laughed.

"Whoa," I turned to Stacy. "And I'm going to assume you know I mean you no harm, but it doesn't matter. Right? It doesn't matter. You have very defined personal space, and even if you're like, 'Come on in, come on in,' I would still want to be aware of that. I want to be aware of where her personal space is. But the same thing can happen, if we're having a conversation and we're talking, I can be paying attention to her physical cues, her facial cues, her energetic cues. All of that can be something that I'm paying attention to. Does that make sense?" I asked the class. "This kind of non-vocal communication is super important, especially because we live in a part of the world where there are lots of different cultures all living together."

"I think also that when you kept walking forward her eyes kind of opened up a little bit," one of the other students mentioned. "Besides going backward, I mean."

"Yep," I agreed.

"She was alert now." One of the other students pushed his hand palm out.

"Someone's in my space. Absolutely. I'll bet that's

what she was thinking," one of the others stated.

"And if someone is in your space, you know it. Right?" I said. "And gentlemen, my apologies in advance," I continued. "Women know it more clearly. Women are far more aware who's in their space most of the time than men are of who's in their space. So, as gentlemen, if you're dealing with a woman, be aware of that. I'm sorry if I sound sexist, but that's how it is. It really just is. Women are more aware."

I paused for a moment and let them digest that information.

"And if you want to relax," I changed direction. "Or you're going to be in a situation where there are people you might not want to deal with, then you want to expand your energy field, and you can do it by doing breathing and visualizing that bubble around you getting bigger."

"You can do that?" Mark, another student asked.

"Absolutely," I answered. "Like we did with this exercise. If you want to expand and include everybody, that's a way to do it. For example, I have a pretty wide field, I'm like, 'Woohoo! Here we are, and this is going to be awesome.' And I'm actually extending my energetic body outwards past this room with my intention. Why? Because I want you all to be super comfortable with what we're doing because some of this is uncomfortable. The more comfortable I can help you be, the more willing you are going to be to take risks. And you're taking some risks right now, so good for you."

I'll tell you what I tell my students: Please start paying conscious attention to other people's energetic bodies and their cues about their space. As you increase your awareness, you will gain insights into how and how closely to connect with others. You will also want to start playing with your energetic body size and distance.

Mission: Energetic Body and a busy restaurant

The next time you are in a busy restaurant, imagine an invisible bubble around you. Make it about two feet in front, behind, above, and below you. Use your imagination and reinforce with the intention that people are not going to cross that envisioned barrier. See what happens. See if people cross it. Note: You might notice that the wait staff doesn't come by either, so don't do this for too long or you'll be waiting a while for your food to come.

Once you see what happens at two feet, make the bubble four or five feet in size. See how everyone reacts to you and the space around you. Take note and remember, you must have the clear intent that you want to have the space set aside for yourself. But make sure you start and stop this exercise. If you don't, you might find that people avoid you or don't see you. Sometimes, that is desirable and sometimes it isn't.

For our purposes, we can use the energetic body to deepen and increase our vocal resonance and presence. We need to fill our energetic body with those sympathetic vibrations that are created in our physical body.

The actual voice box is very small. By itself, it makes a sound that is sort of like a clarinet mouthpiece without the clarinet body – imagine a kind of a squeaky beep and that's pretty much it. On the physical level, if the muscles around the larynx are tight, the voice will sound pinched and squeaky. If they are relaxed and engaged, the voice will sound full and resonant. We must work with both the physical and energetic bodies to make an optimal sound.

Mission: Moving Ah

Stand up. Take a good speaker stance, with your feet hip-width apart and your arms at your sides. Sound the same Ah from before, and as you vocalize the Ah, bring your arms up your sides to shoulder height, and then to that V above your head. You will note that it's louder, of course. But now, we're going to play with moving it quickly from one type of resonance to another.

While you are vocalizing with your arms up in a V over your head, bend your elbows and bring your fingers together so the tips of your fingers touch. Note any change in the quality or characteristics of the sound you're making. Did it change? I'm betting it did. If you didn't notice a change, try it a few more times to get acclimated to what you sound like. If you're having trouble hearing yourself, go ahead and record your voice and listen. Generally speaking, I don't recommend that you record yourself until you have a great deal of speaking experience. Then, absolutely record yourself so you can evaluate how you can improve – but for now, I would prefer it if you went more slowly and trusted what you are hearing live. That's because we hardly ever have a $5000 studio microphone recording us, so we have no good representation of what we sound like. Most readily-available microphones make us sound thin and reedy, and most speakers and amps will not give a fair representation either.

But this one time, turn on the recorder on your phone or on your computer so that you can hear how your sound changes. Play with the elbow-bending portion of the exercise a few times so you get an idea. If you want an explanation, the best one I can give you is that you are changing the size of your energetic body. That's it. You're changing its size. By changing its size, you're changing your instrument size – and the bigger the instrument, the fuller the sound. You'll also change its timbre, characteristics, and quality, which will improve your ability to connect with people and help you shine.

If the voice is the mouthpiece of a clarinet, the rest of the body is the body of the clarinet. The rest of the body and its resonators create the instrument through which the resonance of the voice sounds.

Our physical bodies can do that. And in fact, I'm going to use one of my bandmates as an example. I lead a holiday caroling group called "The Philosopher's Tones." There aren't that many of us, so we have to make four people sound like a choir. One of my bandmates recently lost a large amount of weight – she's literally half the size she used to be. When she was bigger, her voice sounded full, round, and creamy. She had a strong alto and great resonance. Part of why she had so much good resonance was that she had a bigger instrument. The vibrations of her voice suffused her entire body and therefore created more space for the sympathetic vibrations that emanate from the larynx.

Once she was smaller, her voice sounded less full. There just wasn't as much of her to vibrate the sound. So, what is one to do? If you are smaller, and you don't have large resonance chambers like a sizable torso, big sinuses, a large mouth, or a large cranial cavity, you need to use your energetic body.

Your voice goes where you imagine it going. You use your imagination and tell your voice where to resonate, and it obeys. This is a fantastic way to use intent, perception, and the mind/body connection. If we think it, it will happen. Then, we project our voice where we want it to go, and it goes there. It's like our earlier discussion about projecting – the same principles apply inside your body, as well as outside your body. If your body is your instrument, different parts of you will vibrate to different pitches from your larynx. When you employ these projection techniques, you send the sound to the places that are best suited to making the sound bigger and fuller.

If you use your energetic body and project sound out to it, you get a bigger instrument without having to physically be bigger. You suffuse your energetic body with the voice that you are producing. Thus, when my bandmate and I discussed how she could project her voice outside her physical body, her fuller resonance returned in an instant.

Remember the exercise you just did? When you raise your arms, you focus your voice to your arms. The point of that exercise was to show you that it would get louder. And you wouldn't have to do anything to make it so except raise your arms – because when you raise your arms, you are also increasing the size of your energetic body. If it goes about two feet around you and you make it taller and bigger by raising your arms, then instead of being five feet eight or five feet ten, suddenly with your arms up you are ten feet tall. And that makes for a huge instrument through which to sound your beautiful voice.

Eventually, you won't even have to raise your arms to make it work. You'll just have to think about opening up those resonators to suffuse your energetic body with sound, and those vibrations will go wherever you direct them. Play with your energetic body. Change its size and shape with your imagination and intent. Then, speak – and marvel at the difference.

16 THE WRENCH IN THE WORKS

If change is the only constant, then flexibility is the only response. So, what do you do when all hell breaks loose? When the sound system doesn't work, the projector conks out and you're losing the audience by twos and threes? Or you get heckled? Or you lose your voice? Or you've prepared one presentation but it turns out they want something else entirely? What do you do when the entire event throws you nothing but flaming curveballs?

I've been thinking about the importance of flexibility and responsiveness in life and in business. Life does throw us flaming curveballs. Business probably throws them just as often. We must adapt to new situations, needs, and challenges, and when that happens, it's best to be maneuverable. We must be willing to step outside our comfort zones and think of innovative ways to get past our challenges, because let's face it, it's not like the curveballs are going to stop coming.

So, what do we do? How do we deal with the gates of hell bursting open? If something goes wrong, don't react, respond. First, I'd say, get a bird's eye view of the situation. Find a bit of distance and assess the extent of the damage. Then, of course, figure out who can solve the problem if you can't. You can't account for every eventuality, but you can plan for most.

For example, when I'm speaking, I always travel with my own sound system, cables, computer, two thumb drives that contain my notes and presentation, and my own projector, just in case the client's tech blows up. I don't rely on the client to have everything ready. I am particular about my setup, down to where I want my bottle of water to sit while I speak (Don't use a glass if you can at all help it, by the way. They spill, and they break. Instead, bring your own refillable bottle with an easy open spout so you can grab a swig without affecting the flow of your speech too much). Some might say this level of prep is overkill, but I know it's saved me on multiple occasions when the client's equipment malfunctioned.

But there are a lot of things that will be outside your control – all you can control is how you respond to them.

Hecklers

Oh boy! Hecklers. They're so fun. Before I go any further, please note there is a difference between someone who genuinely disagrees and wants to debate you on a topic and a heckler. Someone who has a valid point might warrant a small deviation from your plan. I've stopped a speech to listen and ask a few questions when someone knowledgeable raises an issue. When I don't know the answer to the question they raise, frankly, I say so, and if time allows, I offer to research the point and come back with answer. Or I offer to research it and send out a reply to anyone in the room who wants it. Valid points-of-view can make for a rich and energetic discussion, and that can elevate communication to inspiring heights. I never mind those sorts of interjections. Hecklers, on the other hand, are a different story.

On the rare occasions when a member of my audience heckles me, I fall back on those perception and listening skills we've been practicing. I ask myself "Why? What is making that person raise a fuss?" Usually, they want to prove their intelligence, or they want to spend a little time in the limelight. So, I give it to them. I let them have the spotlight. I celebrate how smart they are for a few seconds. I thank them for bringing up such a fascinating point, and then I move on confidently. Feel free to acknowledge a heckler's viewpoint, but don't take too much time or feed them too much energy. Move along as quickly as possible. More importantly, maintain control of the room. Connect with your audience using some of the techniques I outlined earlier and keep going. After all, you are the person your audience came to hear. Hecklers can try to derail your progress, but you don't have to let them.

In fact, it's good practice and a show of compassion to acknowledge other people's viewpoints in most situations. It's the way we learn from one another. Sometimes, if someone is behaving rudely or in a nasty manner, they are simply hiding a certain amount of pain. And if we can uncover that pain, and better yet, help them deal with it, we might gain a staunch friend and ally. It won't always happen, but I've been surprised at how often it has.

Belligerent Clients

Sometimes, the people you're about to work with have bees in their bonnets, and they get downright rude or belligerent. Of course, if you feel unsafe, take precautions and get out of there. But if you believe you can defuse the situation and still make it a win, you will need to act quickly to figure out what's making them act up.

Were they interested in being the ones who did this themselves? You don't know what's gone on behind the scenes. It's possible this person wanted to make the speech or facilitate the workshop. If so, deputize them. Make them a partner in what you are all doing together, and they'll become your biggest fan. This works incredibly well with misbehaving students – I deputize the greatest troublemaker. I stress the importance of their task, and I give them my faith that they will succeed. In over 20 years of facilitating workshops for students of all ages, I have never had that technique fail.

Do they think what you're doing is bunk? Take a minute and WOW them. Find out what they want, if you can – and then give it to them until they're sated. Often, they don't want things to change too much. They just want to feel like they've had their say and made some sort of impact on the situation. These folks have a lot in common with hecklers, so make them feel important, and maintain control of the situation, and you will appease them. Additionally, if you can honor them and their wishes, even if you're only saying, "I wish I could provide what you're asking for," that can soften an unyielding stance.

In these cases, use your perception skills. For example, if what they want is praise, praise them for burping. If what they want is humor, make them laugh. Often, your clients will be under incredible pressure to succeed, to pull off an amazing event, and they might need something to break their tension and lower their stress level. A self-deprecating joke that helps them laugh can brighten the entire situation and make it feel more manageable to them and to you.

Do you sense the issue has nothing to do with you or the event, but is something in their personal life? Dig deep and find your compassion, and then proceed from that place. It can be super challenging to show compassion to someone who is being nasty. But if you can, you might reap amazing rewards and a connection that lasts far beyond this one occasion. I also recommend that you work with them to deal with the issue they raised with you. Regardless of what might be going on with them internally, resolving this issue will improve their current behavior and perhaps their state of mind.

Are they exhibiting signs of stress? If so, remain calm.

Look for others to work with to bring a peaceable resolution so you can all proceed. Remember, you are a pro. You don't have to put up with people who are being nasty. Having said that, you can also work with them to bring the threat level back down so you can all succeed. Only you can decide for yourself if it is worth it to you to remain and work on it.

Is just one person throwing a wrench into the works? You will find that there are hierarchies in every group of people. There will be the main leader, and hopefully that person is on your side. There will also be factions. You will need to become adept at identifying those factions and figuring out who's the person everyone looks to for their information, ideas, and the lead on how to proceed. If you get that person on your side or at least ready to collaborate with you, you will resolve the issues together and make everything fly.

So whether it's hecklers, cranks or a fuzzed-out sound system, plan for everything to go wrong and prepare for it. Carry extras of everything you will need. Over-rehearse what you will say until about three days beforehand, then stop, and trust yourself to know it. The night before, look it over one last time right before you go to sleep. Where I come from, we do that and then we put the item under our pillow. I'm not saying you have to put your presentation under your pillow after your final read-through – but research suggests that if we peruse something right before we sleep, we will retain more of it the next day. (That's how I memorized the entire multiplication table in one night and aced my test the following day.)

Be prepared to be flexible. Despite a client's best efforts, sometimes things on their end go wrong. Sometimes, other people are late or run long, and you will need to drastically shorten your part. That means you have to know your stuff so well that you can cut and rearrange chunks to suit shorter or longer timeframes. I've struggled with this throughout my career – I can talk forever, but if you ask me to truncate things, I'll try to meet your needs, but I might panic, so I've learned to ask my audience what they want to hear about. It goes something like this: "It turns out we have a little less time than I thought we would," I say. "We're going to have 45 minutes together instead of an hour. So, what do you think I should focus on? What would you like to talk about?"

Once I hear from them, I quickly mentally rearrange my notes and delete a few PowerPoint slides from my deck. And then we're off and running. Sometimes, that means I don't get to do what I planned. Other times, I end up way out of my comfort zone. I view these times as adventures. Don't get me wrong – I do find them stressful, but I also find them fun. I treat this sort of "fly by the seat of your pants" situation as a challenge. And truthfully, once I start and I'm in it, I forget that I'm out of my comfort zone. Instead, I enjoy the ride.

Here's one of my best examples from my own life. Many of my readers and followers know that I have been a tarot card reader for over 35 years. Many people also know that I read palms. I do this for entertainment purposes at corporate events and other places because it helps me connect with people, tell stories, and communicate. There is no greater training for public speaking than reading for 40 different "bosses" at an event, connecting, being accurate, listening, and telling them their tales. It is amazing training, and I still do it every so often.

While most people know my great-grandmother taught me how to read regular playing cards back in the Soviet Union, they don't know how I started doing palm readings. About 17 years ago, I took a corporate job at a lumber company down in Williamsburg, VA., doing tarot card readings for four hours. It was for a corporate holiday event, and I was going to have a table, chairs, and decorations. People would sit down and get their cards read.

I drove the three hours down from Washington D.C. and

showed up to the lumberyard. The DJ at the event also happened to be the booking agent who had contacted my agent to get me to come down and do these readings. When I met her, I asked her where I was going to sit.

"Sit?" she asked. "We don't want you to sit. We want you to do walk-around." (For those who don't know, walk-around is when you go up to the people around the venue and you entertain them with whatever skill they hired you to showcase.)

"I'm not sure I'm going to be able to do tarot card readings while doing walk-around," I said. "Generally I need to be able to lay the cards out."

"I don't want you to do tarot card readings. I want you to do palm readings," she answered.

What?

"I have a contract right here," I produced it. "It doesn't say anything about palm readings," I said. "I'm afraid there's been some mistake. I can't do palm readings tonight because I don't read palms."

"Well, you have to do something. The client wants palm readings."

"I'm sorry. Literally, I don't know how to do them." I excused myself, exited the building, and called my agent.

"We have a problem. They want me to do palm readings."

"Why is that a problem?" she asked.

"Because I don't know how to do them."

"Well, can you do anything?"

"I don't know. I'll try."

This was long enough ago that I had a Handspring Treo. On it, I had a rudimentary palm reading app. I had been meaning to learn how to read palms, but I hadn't gotten around to it. So I went into the ladies' room and spent about ten minutes learning the names of the various lines and mounds of the palm. I figured out which one was the Life Line, which one was the Heart Line and which one was the Head Line. I figured out that the Jupiter mound had something to do with leadership and dynamic qualities. I figured out the Mars mound was about ethics and morals. I did the best I could to figure out what meant what. And then I put the little Treo away, went out to the main room, and proceeded to kick butt reading palms for the next four hours.

How did I manage? Sometimes, I still wonder. But really, the best answer for that is that I had done enough preparation and a sufficient number of readings that I knew how to read the people, their energy, and their lines without even needing to know, consciously, the actual names of things. Because I knew my other material so well and because I was a practiced listener and communicator, I was able to take my knowledge and apply it to a different discipline. In the end, communication is about people, intent, emotion, and energy. If we can figure those out, we can make all the rest work. And I learned a valuable lesson about communication that night which benefits me to this day.

Nowadays, I make sure I get to speak to the clients directly. I no longer take anyone's word for anything. I make sure I get all the information first-hand. Otherwise, I feel I'm being irresponsible and not doing enough to fulfill my clients' needs.

I never again want to be faced with a "What? You came here to teach us how to sing? We didn't want to learn how to sing. We wanted to learn how to twist balloon animals," type of situation. I don't want to hear "We didn't want someone to teach us how to write really great stories. We wanted a magician."

I know balloon animal twisters. I know magicians. If somebody came to me and said that's what they wanted, I would do my best to get them exactly what they wanted. When communication lines are blurred and you're playing a business version of the telephone game, you have to seek clarity.

But even if you try your best and there is no clear path to the correct answer, you have to do what you can. We all have to be adaptable, flexible, and maneuverable in how we solve problems for people. Because let's face it. That's what we do.

We are all in the business of solving other people's problems.

17 WHAT'S YOUR PROBLEM?!

So, how do we do it? How do we give the people who are listening to us what they want, especially when we are ill-prepared to do so? At that lumberyard gig, I was able to bring my previous reading skills and knowledge to bear. But what if you have nothing? Here's the important thing about listening. When what you thought the client wanted turns out to be not what the client wanted at all, you need to engage those listening skills.

No, wait. Let me back up. First, you have to get over your own issues and open your heart, mind, and ears to the other people involved. You must connect with them without your own ego coming to the party. When, a client – or heck anyone – tells you that you're doing something wrong, a certain amount of defensiveness is a natural reaction. If you have ever watched *The Simpsons*, you've probably seen Bart Simpson saying, "I didn't do it. Nobody saw me do it. You can't prove anything." The reason this iconic moment has been repeated so many times during the run of the show is because it's all too common in real life. We want to defend ourselves, because anything else feels like admitting we're wrong. And that can feel terrible. But regardless of how it feels, we have to admit our culpability and fix the problem. We have to get over our insecurities around looking bad or being wrong and make things right. I know, I know. Easier said than done. And yet, we have to, don't we? If we mess up, we have to make amends personally and professionally. Right?

So, if you messed up, it's your responsibility to fix it. That makes sense. However, what if you didn't mess up? What if you're operating in good faith and you've adhered to the conditions and circumstances you knew about and they're still coming at you like you screwed up?

In the moment, it doesn't matter. No one cares. You're stuck in the middle of the situation, and you have to figure out a way to resolve it. And often, an irate client or customer is right in front of you – so not only do you have to take action to fix the problem, you must also be the cooler head.

Think about it this way: Is your goal to be proven right, or is it to serve the other person's needs? And you might be right, no question. You might have the contract, like I did at the lumberyard. You might have an ironclad reason for what you're doing. And still you'll have to deal with the situation at hand. To resolve it and leave everyone happy, you'll need to step back from your initial reaction so you can give a measured response. And that means you have to release the need to defend yourself so you can focus on solving the bigger problem.

When you're in the soup, stop and determine your goal. Take a second and decide your objective. Most importantly, try to do it from an unbiased, dispassionate place. Here's what I do to give myself a second: I change my physical point-of-view. If I'm sitting, I stand, and vice versa. I allow myself to view the issue from a different perspective. That way I can see things differently, and perhaps respond to them differently as well. Additionally, those few seconds of movement provide a moment to breathe and calm my thoughts.

Once I have a bit more peace of mind, I move into problem-solver mode, and I operate from that place until we can fix what's wrong. As part of this process, I remind myself that the issue here is not with me and what I'm bringing to the table. The task at hand is to solve the problem so no one feels like a failure. And if you can solve the problem, you might be the hero of the hour. That's always a fabulous feeling.

So, if you find yourself in a similar situation, try the above perspective-changing technique and see how it works. Even if you know you're right, take a minute to assess what's really going on with the client, then decide whether and how you will help. (Bear in mind that they might not be in a place to appreciate your aid or the fact that you're helping them when you're clearly not at fault. Do this good deed for yourself, regardless of anyone else's actions or reactions. In this scenario, you're here to help. If you can see that there's really no greater reward than that, you will have already won.)

Once you choose to help, you must listen. Dig underneath the surface of what they're saying to the crux of the matter. What do they really want and need? What problem do they want solved? How are they really feeling? Open your senses and figure that out. Once you have an idea of what's going on beneath the surface, you can adapt your skills (and your palm-reading app, if you've got one) to give the client what they want and need. Because remember, just as you're trying to solve their problem, they're trying to solve someone else's, and so on. It's a pretty fascinating daisy chain, isn't it?

When I listened to the DJ/agent at the lumberyard, I had

to go deeper. As soon as I took a moment to assess the situation, I saw the lay of the land. If I tried to fix the issue, I wouldn't just be doing what the end client wanted. I would also be solving a huge problem for the agent as well. At first, I was upset and angry at being placed in this bizarre position of having to seem like an expert at something I had literally never done before. But that wasn't her problem. That was mine. Her problem was that for some reason, she had booked someone her client didn't want, and she was going to have to tell her client that she'd screwed up – so she had an even bigger problem than I did.

After I took a minute to breathe and change my perspective from "Holy crap! I can't do palm readings. I'm going to make a complete fool of myself!" to "OK, how can I help her get out of this sticky situation," I realized I had to try to solve her problem. And as soon as I started listening to her on a deeper level, I got the bigger picture: The agent was super anxious because this lumberyard was one of her bigger clients. She wanted to keep them as clients, and she knew she had screwed up. She told me she didn't care how I did what I did, and begged me to figure out a way to do what the client was asking.

After all, my job was to help and serve. No one had to know I didn't know what I was doing. If I was completely terrible at palm-reading, I was going to fall back on my theatre background and make it all one grand game. The party guests were going to have fun one way or the other. Even if I had no clue how to read palms, I knew how to entertain them, and I did.

I don't know if you've ever seen that wonderful video of Bruce Springsteen and the E Street band pulling Chuck Berry's "You Never Can Tell" out of their hats because someone requested it. If not, here's a link to it.

https://youtu.be/L-Ds-FXGGQg. (The link is also at https://IzoldaT.com/speak-book.) Watch it. You'll see masters at work. Why? It's not just because they're incredible musicians. It's because they're incredible musicians who want so much to satisfy, enthrall, and entertain their audience that they are willing to try a song some of them haven't played for 50 years. To me, that's the amazing thing. Being willing to take a chance to please the others, to excite them, to thrill them by taking that big risk will get you fans for life. Someone knows that you're willing to be vulnerable and perhaps make a grave error and look ridiculous to get them what they need. With that effort, you will earn their trust and win their loyalty. That authentic connection can't be faked, and it can't be bought.

(I'm not comparing myself to Bruce Springsteen and the E Street Band, by the way. They're just another example of a band [practitioner] that collectively wants to please their fans [clients]. And that is crucial.)

So when you end up in this kind of situation, you must decide the kind of risk you're willing to take. And then you have to solve the problem.

Here are the steps to follow.

Step 1: You find out that what you've prepared isn't what the client wants.

Step 1a: Try to make sure the powers that be really want this new thing, or whether there's been a miscommunication somewhere.

Step 2: If it does turn out to be a last-minute change on their part, you have to decide whether or not you're able to address their concerns. You might find that you can't make a change, or you might choose not to make one. If you are super invested in communicating what you prepared, then make that clear, particularly if you have the paperwork to back it up. Make all your apologies and do what you came to do.

Step 2a: You decide you want to work with them and give them what they're saying they want. Excellent! Here's where you get to have some fun. If you're there by yourself, if you don't have colleagues or bandmates, that's even better in some ways. Why? Because you get to think as wild and out of the box as you can.

Step 3: Take a few minutes and speak to the decision-maker. Ask that person exactly what they want, and don't just listen to the words. Listen to what's underneath the words. Listen to the intention. Watch for emotion, for their physical cues. Is this person feeling nervous? Stressed out? If you can determine exactly why they've changed things at the last minute, you can figure out more about how to give them what they want and still do what you came to do.

It's possible that you can modify what you had prepared while still satisfying the new request – in fact, unless you're are a magician and what they want is someone who can teach a master class in opera, you ought to be able to modify by changing your focus.

Bear in mind **you must know your material cold**. If you do, you can take all of the shades, all of the nuance, all of the energy of what you've already got prepared and infuse it into the new theme or subject.

You can color it. You can keep referring back to what they now want, while still talking about what you started with. Here's what I do: I ask myself, if I were the person who knew how to do this cold, what would I say? What are the points I would strike? What are the themes on which I would touch?

Step 4: Take a few minutes of alone time. By the way, did I mention that you need to arrive at any venue at which you are going to be presenting at least a full hour early (and this is only if you have nothing to set up)? If you have any sort of setup, you will need to increase this by a factor of three or four. Things change, and you might find yourself in a situation where the organizer begs you to change everything you had set up. The manner in which you handle those curveballs will build your reputation. Make sure it's the kind of reputation you want.

The most crucial part of working with clients in public speaking or communication situations is identifying what the client actually wants. In the case of the palm-reading gig at the lumberyard, the client wanted everyone to be entertained. They wanted the big boss to get a reading that blew him away. So, I made sure I did that. They wanted people to be amazed. I did that too.

In order to succeed, I had to have enough prep and enough confidence in myself and in my skills to interact on a deeper level. I wasn't nervous or worried, because I knew my stuff. That left me free to connect with everyone on the level where we are all just people with similar needs and desires. Once I tapped into that by listening and sensing what was happening with them, I gave them substantive and accurate readings that amazed them.

My tools? Listen, connect, and communicate from that deep and vulnerable place we all have inside. That was the substance and the key. Everything else was for show. In the end, the evening was a success, but only the first part had been necessary to make it one.

You might want to brainstorm some of this with friends or you might want to brainstorm some of it yourself. In fact, let me get you started. When things have gone sideways with a client, step back, listen, assess, and ask yourself the following questions: "What is it they most want? And what can I do to help them get it?" At every stage, reiterate the question. Ask your client, too – just remember that sometimes, you need to be circumspect in how you ask, and other times you can be explicit.

I sometimes phrase it like this: "So, let me ask you. What is it that you want to achieve here?" And then I watch and listen. I use every sense I can to determine their goal. Were they excited or scared when they related it to me? Were they happy or anxious? If they want something and they're excited about it, you have a ton of leeway and maneuverability to help them get it. If they remain too scared or anxious, they might have other "bosses" to deliver to, and then you have to pay strict attention to how you proceed.

I've been telling you to listen to what the clients want and then give it to them – so now, it's time to learn how to take the information you're receiving and turn it into action. That's a very important lesson. The knowledge and the ability to transform that knowledge into action are two different skill sets, and they are both crucial to success.

18 WHEN THEY'RE WITH YOU – AND HOW TO GET THEM THERE

Certainly, if you know how to give your audience what they want, you've gone a long way to having them in your corner. Sometimes, though, you're asked to speak in situations where you haven't had the chance to do all that research. Has this ever happened to you? Have you been at a wedding or a party and had someone ask you to make a toast or a speech? Daunting? It can be, especially during a raucous party. But I'll tell you what – a raucous party's got nothing on a pitch to a bunch of venture capitalists or a review board. Those are the big leagues. And if you need to speak to a bunch of people like that, you need to know, be, and do more. You need to get to the point where you are dynamic enough, where you speak from such an authentic and engaging place that people can't resist looking at you and listening to you.

This works in every arena: It works if you are a teacher with a class of seven-year-olds, it works if you are a doctor talking with a patient about the following day's surgery, and it works if you are a manager training new employees or letting them go. If you communicate from a place of authenticity, from your gut, your audience will know it. They will know it, and they will respond to it. And that, my friend, is the most important thing.

If you're not getting that response, you might as well be standing in the middle of a forest trying to convince a tree to come with you. It's not going to happen. Trees tend to stay where they are, and if you're trying to convince a tree otherwise, you're on a fool's errand. But when you see them nod their heads, you know you're on the right track. When they smile, you're well on your way. And when they ask questions or blurt out answers or comments, you know they're with you.

And I see that sort of interaction, the blurting of comments and answers and the development of a group discussion as a net positive. I want my audience thinking and asking questions. I want them discussing what we're talking about. I'm delighted when they talk amongst themselves, because I know that in seconds, I can get their attention right back on me and my message. That's because I design my talks to spark curiosity and wonder. And once my audience members are curious, then we can really blast off into new ideas, ways of thinking, and viewing the world. They are active in this exploration, and I am their tour guide. It gets no better than that.

But I don't leave that connection to chance – I work behind the scenes to make it happen.

My Personal Challenge

Before any presentation, I set myself a challenge. I study the people in the audience. I determine which of them least wants to be there. I know that that unwillingness isn't a reflection on me – sometimes, the work I do with companies is mandatory. In that kind of audience, people tend to feel that either they already know what they need to know, or they have deadlines to meet and the event is a waste of their time.

If someone walks in and their energy tells me they don't want to be there, I make it my business to make sure that by the end they won't want to leave. Don't get me wrong – I don't shortchange the people who are all in. But I want everyone to see the transformation in the reluctant folks. If they're vocal in their reluctance at the beginning, I might even nudge them a little and ask them to comment on their about-face towards the end. I want all of us to know how a simple talk can change lives. And if they see that during my presentation, they will be more likely to believe it can happen when they present.

Opportunity to help

The opportunity to help people learn thrills me. When they get it, and I see the light go on, or I hear the questions they've formed because of our discussion, I feel so proud of them. That might be part of the connection we make. It's possible that my enthusiasm for presenting is what's sparking people's interest. But I have a feeling it's more than that. I believe we are all curious beings. Many of us put our curiosity aside so that we can get our daily work done. And yet that curiosity about ourselves, each other, and the content makes it easier to connect. So, our mission as communicators is to discover what sparks the audience's curiosity. Then, we must ignite it.

It also helps if we figure out what they want and then focus our talk on those exact themes. And I don't mean that you should talk exactly about their desire ("So I hear you all want a promotion," or "I understand you are all looking to get married."). I mean that you should address your subject through the lens of their desires. **Nothing perks up our ears like hearing about how we might get something we want.**

This is another instance where doing your research is absolutely necessary. If you are addressing a group of sales reps, you might look into the problems they face as they do their jobs. What would they most like to address? And how can your presentation alleviate some of those issues?

For example, if their customers are leaving their brick-and-mortar locations to do business online, a presentation that focuses on providing a personalized and customized touch would be more effective than one that focuses on all of the things that the internet can do for us. On the other hand, if these are people who work mainly online, then you want to look at how the Internet can help them thrive. Tailor what you say and how you say it to what they most need to hear, and you will be golden. If you can work on their problems and desires as part of your communication with them, if you've focused your presentation on building trust, you'll go a long way towards helping them engage with you.

The same thing goes for your interactions in interviews. If you are applying for a job, they're going to ask you all sorts of questions about your experience and your background. You can expect that. However, you can tailor your answers to address what your potential bosses most need to be done. Remember, **we are all in the business of solving other people's problems**. So, if you know that what they most need is a creative thinker who can operate outside any box, you will answer those questions from that perspective and through that lens.

I hope this makes sense – because we can no longer afford to tell clients only what we know how to do. We must communicate to them that what we know will benefit them. Again, I'm not saying you should ever lie. If you can refocus what you communicate through the lens of what they most need, you won't have to lie. You will be telling the whole truth, only through a specific filter. And since this filter addresses what they need, it will be to everyone's benefit.

Staying Present: Physically, Mentally, and Vocally

In any of these situations, remember to keep your voice resonant. Keep your breathing deep and slow, even if you are excited. Let other clues show your excitement. Lean forward, widen your eyes, and let your body language communicate your enthusiasm. Regardless of how excited you are on the outside, stay calm and alert on the inside. Your calm-yet-alert status will keep your voice from rising and from sounding strained, reedy, or thin.

It may sound contradictory, but you can be calm *and* excited. There's a difference between excited and nervous – the former is ebullient, the latter is anxious. Ebullience will heighten the energy in the space. The anxiety will darken it.

Whether you are presenting to a group, going on an interview, or speaking to a packed house, you can apply the above techniques in any speaking situation. They work particularly well when you are presenting to groups or facilitating any sort of workshop. Often you will have brochures, information packets, PowerPoint decks or other materials for them to review. However, frequently, people pay little attention to those once they can watch and listen to a live person.

Regardless of the information you're presenting, your audience will want to hear and see you more than they pay attention to any of those supplemental items. After all, you're live and in person. That beats paper or a PowerPoint deck any day of the week. In this way, you're the star of the show regardless of the information you want to convey.

Some of the workshops I facilitate have no visual aids; they work better if I don't use them. Sometimes, I do need to use them and I am happy to do it if the need arises. But again, don't use them as a crutch. Use them as a supplement, as the icing on top of a delicious cake.

You might be asking yourself, "But what about if you have a whole bunch of data to show? And what if the data isn't the most exciting in the world?" These are excellent questions. Here are some things to ask yourself as you develop your talk and presentation: What about the data is compelling? What story does it tell? How can you make that story relevant to the people listening? What message do you want them to hear?

Let's say you are standing in front of a lot of people to talk about the rainfall numbers in the Pacific Northwest of the USA. On the surface, it might not seem like a scintillating topic. Until …

Until you think about the data in a different way. Idaho, Washington, and Colorado all grow the bulk of potatoes in the USA. And we all know what that means. People like me need potatoes. Badly. We need them because we need French fries, and if we don't have appropriate rainfall to grow lots of potatoes, the French fry eaters might be broken-hearted. So, if I had to talk about rainfall in the Pacific Northwest, my first words wouldn't be, "I'm here to talk to you about rainfall in Idaho." My first words would be, "Who here likes French fries?"

I guarantee a lot of hands will go up. And then you've got them!

19 PREPARATION

Let's discuss tactics. How do you prepare for the different scenarios in which you will be communicating? Meetings, interviews, or public speaking events – you'll practice and prepare for each differently, although there are some commonalities.

I realized something recently: I no longer practice to make it perfect. I practice to make it peaceful. I don't need to be perfect in my talks or workshops. I need to be prepared, and I need to be authentic. When I am real with my participants, we can get to the business of learning and growing much more quickly than if I am perfect. **Perfect intimidates. Real liberates.**

Thus, when you prepare for any sort of communication, aim for authenticity more than perfection.

Meetings

The key here is research. Before you head into the meeting, ask for a list of the attendees. Research them beforehand. Knowing something about them and being able to establish that you've got something in common will help both of you – it will put you at ease, and it will show them you care enough to be prepared. As I said above, when you're communicating with someone, make sure you are calm but excited. That means you need figure out for yourself how to get to that state – but at the very least, remember to breathe. (And don't let the other people in the room get you riled up.)

Head over to the Proper Breathing Technique Deep demo video, [https://youtu.be/gotwRRy7KBE or see the website, https://IzoldaT.com/speak-book under the Chapter 19 heading], for a simple tutorial on how to breathe properly so you project confidence, calm, and peace. This technique will ensure you have enough breath in your body so your voice comes out resonant and strong. The physical aspects of preparing for a meeting mean that you sit properly both to carry yourself well and to feel more confident and present. I won't get physical here, because other people have done better jobs than I at that. However, make sure you do take a few moments to stand in the Wonder Woman or Superman pose (feet shoulder-width apart, hands on your hips, shoulders back, and eyes looking forward) before you walk into the meeting room. It might feel silly, and it might also give you a little added energy.

Shake hands firmly if you're in a culture that shakes hands. Some cultures do not shake hands, so it's up to you to learn where they're from and take your cues from them. Don't sit until invited to do so. And when you do sit, remember to breathe. Be sure to wear clothes that will not constrict your ability to take deep, slow breaths while you are sitting down. This is very important, because when something is constricting your belly, you will have a tougher time breathing and exuding confidence. Worse, you might feel lightheaded. The second you are lightheaded, your brain works less efficiently, and the longer you stay lightheaded, the more your body concentrates on getting good, solid breaths. All of the other processes take a backseat. You might also flush. If your breathing becomes more rapid because you're not getting enough air, the blood will come to the surface, your heart will pump harder and your breaths will be shallow.

Are you starting to get the picture? If you get red-faced and anxious, it becomes a self-fulfilling prophecy and a vicious circle. The more anxious you are the shallower your breaths will be. And if you take shallow breaths, you will also become more anxious.

Another thing that changes when you have insufficient breath and breath support is your voice. Your voice gets shaky. It can get whisper soft. It can shudder. You might stutter. In short, you won't have what you need to sound confident, calm, and like you know what you're doing.

The best thing to do in that situation is to stop for a few seconds and take a couple of deep breaths. While you're doing that, you look pensive and that works just fine. If you can take that moment to do some thinking about what you need to say next, so much the better.

And if the pitch of your voice rises when you are nervous or anxious, one fantastic way to counter that is to nudge your voice down into your chest. Breathe deeply and roll your shoulders back, and engage your pectoral muscles. Then, open your mouth and speak. If you believe your voice will still feel shaky, ask a short question and then breathe while it is being answered. Full breaths and engaged abdominal muscles will help your voice stay strong and solid.

To stave off nerves and anxiety, get into the habit of doing daily breathing exercises, like the ones in the video above. They will be quick and painless, and they will help.

And if you need to calm down, but you literally only have a minute, try my Find Your Calm video: https://youtu.be/5iU1Jq30BHY. (You can also find it at the website.) Use it before any meeting, interview, or speech. It will revolutionize your performance.

One last bit of guidance: Find out how formal the company or organization is. Then, be one level more formal. Some organizations are warm and friendly, and some have a more regimented atmosphere. Gauge it beforehand, and you will have a better idea of how to interact and engage your counterparts so the occasion is a successful one.

Presentations

If you're going to be presenting, get as much information as possible beforehand (do you sense a theme here?). Know how many people will attend. Know their general demographics (age, education level, interests, background, etc.), their professions, and if possible, how they like to spend their time. Remember, you want to know as much as you can so you can tailor your remarks to make the most impact. The more you know, the better you will prepare. Get into the space early and pick out your focus points, the areas you'll be projecting to. Look for the corners and test out speaking/presenting to them. It goes without saying that you should be prepared to go on even if your computer fritzes out, or your entire PowerPoint deck disappears in a puff of smoke right in the middle of your presentation. Know your stuff cold. Be able and willing to work from memory and to improvise – that will also help you answer any oddball questions the audience lobs your way. And don't wait for an emergency to show them you know your stuff. Know your topic. Learn the latest trends. Do your research and then "wow" your audience, because that will help them accept you as an expert. Just be aware that you can't know everything, so have the humility and willingness to learn. I can't tell you how many times my students' wisdom has floored me; a stray comment or question can change perspective and reveal the miraculous to the person willing to see it.

A quick aside: The PowerPoint Deck

Some speakers rely on PowerPoint decks in order to make their point. Let's look at the name PowerPoint. It means that it helps you point, or make your point powerfully. That's fabulous. And I don't think it's a bad thing, particularly since many audience members might learn visually rather than via audio. They might need images in order to process what you're saying.

However, PowerPoint and other visual aids should complement or supplement what you're communicating. They should not be the crutch upon which you lean in order to state your case or persuade an audience to your point of view.

If you want to engage your audience, your body, voice, and energy ought to be enough. Of course, they aren't always going to be – I would never tell you not to use visual or audio aids at all when you are communicating or presenting. They can be super effective.

You can find tons of information on how to create an effective and successful PowerPoint deck, so I won't spend too much time on it – but here are a few tips.

1. Mostly images
    a. Graphics that explain and entertain
2. Few words
    a. Size 32 font or bigger
    b. Contrasting colors
    c. Don't use lots of reds as they fatigue the eye
3. Refer to the slides but don't read them.
    a. Know them cold
    b. They are supplements to what you are saying not the text of what you're saying.
    c. Use them to make points and to entertain
    d. Refrain from using them as a crutch. You will thank me for this one when the power goes out. I promise.
4. Spend no more than two minutes per slide
    a. If you are doing a twenty-minute presentation and you want to leave five minutes for questions, have no more than seven slides.

See an example at https://IzoldaT.com/speak-book under Chapter 19.

Some people don't use slides or other audio-visual aids at all when they present. I like them, because I believe we all learn differently. Some of us are auditory learners. We learn by hearing and we don't need or want to see anything written. Some of us are more visual – if we see it, we grok it. And some of us are kinesthetic learners who need to be part of the movement or the flow of learning. If you come across a bunch of those folks, be prepared to have activities you can all do together. Get them up and get them moving – they will love it, and you will succeed.

When I present or facilitate workshops, I combine all three ways of learning. We interact and discuss. We have visuals to help tell the tale. And we get up and at 'em to seal the deal. That combo knocks it out of the park. Every time.

If you want help or ideas on how to incorporate activities and movement into your workshops, head over to IzoldaT.com/movement for a bunch of tools to get you started.

Interviews

What is your role when you walk into an interview? Who are you? What are you planning to accomplish? Are you excited? Nervous? Confident? Terrified? Professional? Idealistic? You can be a combination of all of those, but you don't have to show anything on the surface that you don't want to show. How cool is that!

Sure, the "real you" might be quaking in your boots. But, what if you were to assign yourself the role of someone who is confident, competent, and a compelling communicator? What if you decided you're the perfect candidate, but the person interviewing you just doesn't know it yet? How might that feel? Try it on for size. Go stand in front of a mirror, and say this to yourself a few times:

"I am a confident, competent, compelling communicator, and I am ideal for this position. That is my role. I will be playing the role of someone who is perfect for this."

Say the words, Say them three times, at least, into the mirror. Make eye contact with yourself. You might even dare to smile as you say that.

Here's the magic: If you believe it, it will work!

See, I'm not writing this book for all of the people out there who can already stand up on any stage and shout, "Here I am, world!" I'm writing it for the rest of us. I'm writing it for those of us who might be hiding a brilliant supernova under a bushel, because we are too shy or too hesitant to speak up.

If we are not naturally extroverted, if we don't have the gift of gab, but we find ourselves needing to behave as if we do, we must know the tips and tricks that will get us through until we are ready to take center stage fully in our own skin.

Again, don't get me wrong – I'm not telling you to be disingenuous. I'm saying you should walk in there as you – but as you do, throw on the cloak of your innermost confident and competent self. Before you go into that interview (or meeting or presentation), arm yourself with the knowledge that you've got this! And always remember that fabulous question: "If I were a person who was confident, competent, and a compelling communicator, what would I do?"

Answer that question for yourself. Your answer will be different from mine, but it will be no less effective. I've presented in front of ambassadors, celebrities, politicians, and first-graders – some of the toughest audiences in the world. And if I am ever doubtful about my abilities, I answer that question for myself before I start. If it helps, make a list of the answers and keep it in your pocket. Glance at it when you need it. Give yourself all the help you need to allow yourself to shine.

See, I know we all have it within us. I am as certain of that as I am that the sun will rise tomorrow.

20 SUBJECTIVE AND OBJECTIVE TRUTH

If we are authentic with our audiences, we all win. No one is pulling the wool over anyone's eyes. Objectively, we all emerge victorious because we all know the truth. Here is the thing, though. The truth can vary. Weird, right? But it can. The truth splits into two or three strands – think of the saying: There's your side, my side, and the truth. You could also define it as subjective and objective truth.

To me, subjective truth is the truth as each individual person experiences it. That's the trouble with these philosophical discussions. We can say something is an objective truth, and we might all agree on that objective truth. And then someone comes along and says, "No, that's not how it is at all. You have all believed incorrectly all these years." Let's look at the idea of a flat Earth. For a long time, people just knew the Earth was flat, until someone came along and said that what they had believed was an objective truth was subjective to them because they were working from a flawed sense of their own perspectives (their subjective truth).

Then, the new truth came into play. And are we now more certain that a round Earth is an objective truth? I am sure, but some people still aren't. And that causes issues in discussing the matter, because every person's idea of truth differs at least a little.

Let's look at the color of an oak leaf. You and I and a million other people can all agree that an oak leaf is green, right? Is that an objective truth? First, let's look at it from the perspective of someone who is red/green colorblind. They might be able to agree that an oak leaf is green, but their experience of that green will be entirely different from someone who is not colorblind. Plus, we must look at how each individual's eyes perceive the color. Can we know that we are each seeing the same color green? Even if we compare the leaf to a color chart, and we all choose the same swath of color as the green we see, are we all really seeing the same green at all? How do we tell?

And what about the people whose eyes show them a slightly different shade of green? Are they objectively wrong? How do we decide? At that point, does the majority rule on the color of the leaf? And if that is the case, isn't that then just a bunch of people's subjective truth?

Here's another example. Objectively, we know gravity works, right? But what would happen if it no longer did? For now, we know it keeps working. Does that make gravitational pull an objective truth? Or is it subjective because each being feels the pull of that gravity differently? Certainly, an elephant has a different perspective of the truth of gravity than does a bird or a butterfly.

I don't disagree there is likely only one truth. But we all approach that "One Truth" from myriad perspectives. Therefore, how can we ever know whose version of the truth is absolute? As soon we bring thinking beings into any equation, we also bring perspective. That, by definition, makes everything subjective, because we are all different. We all think and perceive differently through our senses, and that's why, even if we strongly disagree, we still need to respect differing opinions and other people's versions of the truth. I might not agree with you, but I owe it to you to respect what you say, even as we argue against each other's viewpoints.

As I delve further into ideas on communication, perception, and perspective, I am becoming increasingly aware that the way we communicate is evolving. Likely, a fair number of factors are driving these changes. I could offer that the prevalence of social media, immediate connectivity, and the rise of "fake news" have changed our entire communication landscape. Although I'm not certain exactly what is responsible for this change, I see it happening. Even as I recognize this evolution, I maintain that as communicators, we are better served to respect others' opinions, thoughts, and ideas.

When we present or speak in public, we must be conscious of these differing views and approaches to the truth. Certainly, we are responsible for getting our message across. But if, while we're doing it, we trample on the beliefs, or subjective truths, of others, then we lose before we've begun.

I'm not advocating that you water down your message. But I do want you to be aware – and stay aware – of the opposing views, for several reasons. First, that awareness will help you be more empathetic and considerate of your audience. Second, you can let it inform your presentation. Finally, you can connect with people you understand better than those who remain a mystery.

Think of it as reaching across the cosmic aisle. When we do that, we increase the connection and engagement of everyone in the space. And when we are trying to communicate with people, that makes all the difference in the world.

21 GRATITUDE

Last, but so very not least, I need to talk about gratitude. Entire books have been written all about how grateful we should be to the moon, the stars, the sun, the cashier, and the person who picks up our dog's poop. We are told that the law of attraction works if we are grateful in advance.

And here's the thing. It's all true. The reason we have so many books and self-help gurus talking about gratitude is that it is an optimal way to live. All of the other ways seem to end up with us learning harsh lesson after harsh lesson until we finally learn gratitude.

So what does gratitude have to do with communication, public speaking, interviews, and meetings? I'm glad you asked.

On a fundamental level, if you're giving a speech, there's a lot to be grateful for. People have gathered with the intention of benefiting from what you are going to say to them. They are willing to listen to you. They are willing to open themselves and their minds, and perhaps even their hearts and souls to hear your message. Someone who gives you their time and attention deserves your gratitude. You have the chance to connect on some deep and intimate levels with the people who listen to you.

In a meeting or interview, the same thing holds true. Certainly, in an interview, the need for gratitude exists – but I'm not saying you should be grateful just for the chance at a job. Instead, I believe we can be grateful for the chance to connect with someone who has surpassed us in experience. Remember, when you are in any kind of communication situation, you are there to listen and learn as well as to speak – and maybe more to listen and learn.

Here's a quick gratitude meditation for you.

Meditation: Gratitude

Sit back in a chair, close your eyes, deepen your breathing like we talked about before, and imagine or think the following words:

"I am grateful for the opportunity to connect, communicate, listen, and learn with [person x]." Repeat that three times. Take a deep breath before each time you say it. As you inhale imagine yourself taking in serenity and peace. As you exhale, breathe out gratitude.

Personal relationships also benefit from gratitude during communication. What better time to be grateful than when you and your friends and loved ones can speak and listen to each other? When we feel heard, we draw closer together, and we feel valued and honored. If someone discounts your thoughts, that can be devastating, particularly if you are attempting to communicate during a vulnerable moment. Offer gratitude to yourself for being vulnerable and courageous enough to speak out. Offer that same gratitude to the other person for their willingness to listen and to hear you. That connection, that intimacy, will work wonders.

LAST THOUGHTS

One last note from me: My loves, I am grateful for your attention and your courage in pushing your boundaries. I hope this book has provided insight and actionable techniques on how to thrive in the world of connection and communication. If we remember that communication and self-expression are our birthrights, we will keep speaking up honestly. If we remember that we are all one people, we will keep reaching out and connecting authentically. If we remember to listen, we can learn the secrets to happiness, wisdom, and peace.

Ultimately, the best way I have found to communicate honestly and authentically is to practice. I reach out to friends and strangers. I engage with people I don't know in the hope that we will cease to be strangers. We will instead share an instant of connection that will give us all a spark of hope.

I believe that this form of listening communication is key to saving the world. It is the vital piece that can turn strangers into friends and enemies into allies. If we can talk to each other – and more importantly, listen to one another, we can't remain strangers. That moment, that instant we seek out and find the light in others is when we make the magic that can change everything.

This possibility fills me with admiration for all of you who have embarked on this challenging and rewarding path. I hope to connect with you and cheer you on as you walk it. Until then, I send you all my love.

Izolda

APPENDIX A

Give them what they want. For real.

Here's an excerpt from one of my Speak From Within workshops that'll help you get an idea of the importance of clear communication and giving your audience what they want so you can all succeed.

–Begin Excerpt–

I have a great story about communicating clearly. One day, I was chatting with Dean O'Keefe (not his real name), one of the chief scientists for the Earth Observatory at NASA, and he told me that he and his wife were exact opposites in their personalities and in their communication styles.

One evening, he was driving home and he passed a fruit cart, so he bought some peaches. When he got home, he walked into the house and said, "Honey, I brought home some peaches. Do you want one?"

"I haven't had peaches in years," she replied from the bedroom.

"So do you want a peach, or do you not want a peach?" he asked. You see, in his mind, she could have been saying "I haven't had peaches in years, how fabulous," or "You know I'm allergic to peaches, I haven't had a peach in years." And he could not figure out which one she meant. He needed the answer to be clear-cut. He told me that his wife's tone of voice and inflection didn't provide any information because he needed a definitive verbal answer. Regardless of how his wife inflected her response, her "I haven't had peaches in years" was meaningless to him.

Here's what would have worked: "Would you like a peach?"

Either "Yes." or "No," would have been effective answers. Does that make sense? It's an unusual thing, but it's something to think about. We must figure out what people want, and then we have to give it to them in the way they want it. And more importantly, make sure it's something you're ready to give.

"Let's try an exercise," I continued. "Go ahead and stand up. There are eight of you, so if four of you can be on this side of the room and four of you stand on that side of the room. I'm going to ask you to do something. I'm going to ask you, by whatever method you can, get one of the people from the other side of the room to cross over to you. And the thing is, you don't want to cross over – but see what you can do to get one person to cross the room to your side."

[For the next few minutes, the participants attempted to talk each other into crossing the imaginary line. No one did. They stopped talking for a moment.]

"Is that it? You've given up?" I asked.

"No!" they all shouted.

"Things just got interesting," I nodded. "Okay. Anybody else?"

"Why don't you just come over? This side is better."

"Why is that side better? Do you think they're going to trust you about that?" I asked.

"Sometimes, it's better to just ask," a participant said.

"And see what happens?" I asked.

"They can say no."

"Okay."

"So come over here and show me your beautiful new bracelet."

"No."

"Will that work?" I asked. "Do you want to go show her the bracelet?"

"No."

"Why not?" I asked.

"Because I don't want to cross over."

"OK," I said. "You don't want to cross over. So no one has given anybody else any sort of reason to cross over to the other side yet?"

"Not a good reason, anyway."

"OK, then," one of the participants brandished the keys to his car. "Take my car."

"What!" We all turned to him.

"Take the car. If you come over this side and take the key, it's yours!"

"Do you mean it?" I asked.

"I mean it."

"You'll give them your car?"

"It's a BMW, and I'll give it to them."

"Really. For real?"

Several of the participants on the other side of the room from him started walking towards the line.

"I'm not sure about this," he backed up. "I can't handle it."

"OK, so that's not happening," I said. "Anyone else?" I gestured to the rest of the room.

"Come over to this side. I've got the answer key to the mid-term."

"No, you don't."

"I do."

"Where is it?"

"Um." He halted.

"That's the thing," I said. "You went for an unrealistic offer because you don't have the answer key, do you?

"No, I don't."

"So it wasn't a real reason."

"Does it have to be?"

"Oh, it's a got to be a real reason," I said.

"So was it authentic?" I continued. "Well, because realistically speaking, just like I know I can't put my fingers through this table, chances are I know that you have not gotten the midterm exam. And we all know it, right?"

"And that's important." I turned to the man who was still holding his car keys. "And you said, 'I want to put up my car.' And you know what? They're not going to take it. And I know that and so do you. So, what are we doing in this experiment? What can we do to convince someone? You were thinking, 'Okay. I'm going to go bigger. I'm going to double down, or triple down, and give my car to the first person who comes across the line.' And did anyone believe him?" I turned to the rest of the group.

"'No,' we all thought. 'I can't believe he's going to do that. There's no way.' So nobody took the inauthentic offer." I pulled two one-dollar bills from my purse. "Now, here's a perfectly authentic offer. I have $2 to the first person who comes over."

"Yeah, heck, yeah. I'll take it." One of the participants crossed the line.

"Is that real, though?" One of the others asked.

"Yeah," I answered. "It's real. It's realistic. It's authentic. Here's your $2." I handed her the bills.

"Shoot! That's right. Why wasn't I standing on that side?" one of the participants laughed.

"But do you all see? All of a sudden, it's an authentic offer, and I'm not going to go, 'I need my $2 back.' This is your $2. You went, 'Okay, let's go.' And you got it. And it's an important lesson for all of us to be authentic communicators. If you offer up something that you can't back up, if you say, 'I'm going to offer you the moon,' you'd better have the moon up your sleeve and then some. You want to under-promise and over-deliver. You don't want to say, 'I'm going to give you a loan. Actually, all I've got is this pen.' Instead, you want to be able to make offers that are authentic and doable, in any interaction."

"In that moment," I turned to the woman who got the two dollars. "You thought, 'Heck yeah, I'll take the money. Let's go.' Why? What made you think it was an OK thing to do?"

"I guess I figured that you meant it."

"Did I give you any reason to think that I didn't?"

"No."

"And it wasn't unrealistic. I didn't say, '$10,000 to the first person who comes over.'"

"That's unrealistic."

"What was that?" I asked.

"That is unrealistic."

"Yes. That would be unrealistic. But my offer of the two bucks was concrete, and it was deliverable. It was immediate and authentic. So, it was super easy to say, 'I'll take it.'"

– End Excerpt –

Whenever you communicate, be authentic and realistic. Only promise what you can deliver. And then deliver just a little bit more.

This last idea is key. If you are not authentic, you might win in the short-term, but in the long-term, you will lose. Why? Because your audience will learn that you aren't real, and they will check out. So, if you want them with you and eager for your next bit of wisdom, be truthful with them. It's the only way you all will win.

APPENDIX B

Whenever I teach one of my communication seminars or workshops, I ask the participants for their definition of what makes a good communicator.

Here are some of the answers they have given me over the years:

- Confidence: In yourself and your ability to speak and present
- Charisma: Making a good impression. General friendliness
- Knows the customs: Social norms like eye contact, handshakes and eye contact
- Knowledge: Know the topic cold
- Articulate/audible: Can we hear you and understand you?
- Good listener/active listener: Able to reflect during communication
- Awareness of body language: Yours and theirs
- Self-awareness: Know yourself and your interior landscape
- Sense of humor: Judiciously applied

- Developed kinesthetic sense: Awareness of where people are in space
- Able to improvise: Able to change direction and modify mid-stream
- Sympathetic: Able to feel concern for other people
- Empathetic: Able to put yourself in their shoes
- Caring and Concerned: About the welfare of others
- Considerate: Aware of the needs of others/listeners
- Melodious voice: Easy to listen to, well-modulated, non-monotone
- Non-confrontational (unless confrontation is called for): Able to see multiple viewpoints in a given situation

Refer to the above skills whenever you need to communicate or present. You can exhibit any one of these, and chances are you will succeed in your efforts. If none of them work, stop and ask yourself this one question: "What is one thing I can do, right now, to make things better?"

Ultimately, if you are at a loss and things have careened downhill in the middle of a presentation, stop and breathe. Then, ask your audience the same question.

"What do you all think? What is one thing I can do right now, to make things better?" In such situations, if the audience has seemed amenable, I've even asked them how we could improve things together.

One time, at a show, a thunderstorm knocked out the power minutes before I was due on stage. I had no amplification, no lights, and three hundred people who wanted a show.

"Who has flashlights?" I called to the group. Several people answered yes.

"OK, I'm making all of you my roadies," I said.

We got everyone seated directly in front of me, and the "roadies" shone their lights on me while I sang and played. The rain was beating on the tin roof and lent some wonderful percussion to my performance.

The entire audience and I pulled together to make it a magical and memorable occasion. It was a blast. So, now, I never hesitate to ask my audiences to get in on the act. Usually, they love being part of the show.

You and your audience can get the same incredible results. If issues crop up, ask for ideas and get help. Your audience will love having a role. Together, you can brainstorm and come up with an answer superior to one any of you would have thought up on your own. Remember, we're all in this together – both the communicators and the audience.

ABOUT THE AUTHOR

Born in the former Soviet Union, Izolda conquered language barriers and a public-speaking phobia to become a heart-centered, engaging communicator. As part of the year-long immigration process, she and her family lived in a war zone. During that time, she began to develop her unique strategies to manage stress through the body/mind connection. She traveled internationally for NASA teaching professors, scientists, diplomats, and business leaders how to teach and communicate their message. She speaks on leadership, creativity, and stress management. She also presents leadership, communication, and creativity programs in the USA and all over the world. She lives in Greenbelt, MD with her husband, dog, and two cats. She holds a BA in English from the University of Michigan. She loves to travel. She has a mission to visit one new country every year and meet as many new people as possible.

Connect with Izolda
Speaking and Programming: https://IzoldaT.com
Author Website: http://IzoldaTWriter.com
Podcast: Tell Your Story Better: Communication Made Simple

Books by Izolda

Non-fiction
- Life Elements: Transform Your Life with Earth, Air, Fire, and Water
- Rock the Hand You're Dealt

Fiction
- The Fiddler's Talisman, Book One of the Fairy Godmother Diaries
- The Piano's Key, Book Two of the Fairy Godmother Diaries

Get in touch. I hope to hear from you.

Made in the USA
San Bernardino, CA
15 September 2018